CW00905445

Collins

Need to know?

Writing Fiction

Collins

First published in 2007 by Collins
an imprint of HarperCollins Publishers
77-85 Fulham Palace Road
London W6 8JB

www.collins.co.uk

A catalogue record for this book is available from the British Library

Text: Alan Wall
Writing exercises: Gill Paul
Editor: Grapevine Publishing Services Ltd
Typesetter: Judith Ash
Series design: Mark Thomson

ISBN 978-0-00-724435-5

Printed and bound by Printing Express Ltd
Hong Kong

Contents

Introduction 6

1 **All about character** 8

2 **Plot** 26

3 **Setting** 38

4 **Good writing** 46

5 **The short story** 64

6 **The novel** 82

7 **Irony** 96

8 **Humour in fiction** 106

9 **Themes, motifs and modes** 116

10 **Some practicalities** 164

Further information 178

Select bibliography 180

Useful websites 181

Useful addresses 182

Acknowledgements 182

Glossary of fictional terms 183

Index 190

Introduction

Fiction is the creation of character and narrative in prose. Theatre and cinema have images and music; they even have holograms and special effects. Radio at least has the intonations of an actor's voice, to beckon and cajole. Fiction relies entirely on the written word as it is presented to the reading eye on the page. In this lies its enormous freedom, and its peculiar difficulties. There is nothing in principle that the fiction writer cannot do. The writing must be accomplished though, or the reader will soon be lost.

Ancient writers used to say that fiction stood midway between history and fable. It employs the inventiveness of legend but must make itself convincing by use of that historical element which produces a kind of 'realism', even in the modern form of writing called 'magic realism'. In a fairy story, a giant eagle can swoop out of the sky and carry away our hero to a safer land. If the modern writer of fiction is to employ the same device then there can be no automatic reliance upon the reader's acceptance or credulity.

Fiction must convince, and it achieves this by the skilfulness of the writing, and the sense of localized reality it generates. The means by which such skilfulness might be achieved are the subject of this book. *Writing Fiction* does not make any pretence to being exhaustive, since it could not possibly be so. What it does is to try to cover some of the techniques required for any serious writer of fiction today.

Fiction creates an imaginary world. It may be only a cameo of a world, as in a short story. It may be an enormous, panoramic world with multiple characters, the sort we find in George Eliot or Tolstoy. It may be a world of considerable external activity, as in *Gulliver's Travels* or *Tom Jones,* or one of unrelenting interiority, as with much of Samuel Beckett's later writing. Sometimes it is obsessed with war, sex or history. It may be set in the past, as a great deal of contemporary writing is; or it may be set in the future, like much of the work we normally refer to as science fiction. This last term is not a very helpful one, since much futuristic writing is relatively unconcerned with science. But we are stuck with it, and will use it here, referring to this type of writing from now on as SF.

An imaginary world convinces us of its verisimilitude – its truthfulness within its own form – by the specific gravity of its characters and the different aspects of fiction writing which allow the writer to shape such an imaginary world successfully. We will look at such aspects of fiction writing as character, plot, voice, setting, humour and irony. We will look carefully at the writer's use of language. This is, after all, our medium; lack of attention here would be fatal. We are shaping worlds and we do it with words.

1 All about character

The fiction writer can go anywhere, be anyone, travel in an instant to the other side of the world or even to another planet. But the writing must have weight. The words on the page must have substance, or the reader will not believe that they actually convey the reality of anyone at any time. Fiction explores its realities through the probing and exposition of character, so one of the first steps for a writer is to think about how to create believable characters.

All about character

We read fiction to enter a new world; and we write it to create one. Fiction is a way of exploring reality through invention. Let's start, logically enough, with ways of establishing the characters who are going to tell us the story.

must know

Where to begin?

Start writing wherever the interest is greatest; always try to write out of passionate concern, since this tends to produce the best prose. It does not matter whether or not this will end up as 'the beginning'. When the beginning must finally be composed (often towards the end of the writing process, in fact) it needs to be striking, succinct and enticing. Remember: it is on the basis of this that the reader will or will not proceed.

Beginnings

The beginning of any work of fiction is an announcement. In a sense it is even an annunciation. A curious unknown creature enters the room of our life and changes the narrative tone of everything. That's what any 'new beginning', any story or novel, does inside the room of our minds. A door opens and a different voice is heard for the first time. Everything suddenly changes. Our new world has arrived.

For this reason, the beginning of any piece of fictional writing is crucial. Its achievement – or lack of it – will decide whether we are to continue or not. This entry into our lives, this sudden consciousness of an unknown voice, an unfamiliar story, a different account of things, is asking for our time. So what does it offer in return? Let us look at a few famous openings and see what they put before us.

Here is the beginning of Herman Melville's *Moby Dick*:

Call me Ishmael. Some years ago – never mind how long precisely – having little or no money in my purse, and nothing particular to interest me on shore, I thought I would sail about a little and see the watery part of the world. It is a way I have of driving off the spleen, and regulating the circulation. Whenever I find myself growing grim about the mouth; whenever I find myself involuntarily pausing before coffin warehouses, and bringing up the rear of every funeral I meet; and especially whenever my hypos get such an upper hand of me, that it requires a strong moral principle to prevent me from deliberately stepping into the street, and methodically knocking people's hats off – then, I account it high time to get to sea as soon as I can.

Ishmael wants us to be on first-name terms. The very first sentence of the book is an invitation to intimacy. But note how much information we are given in this opening; see how much we find out about Ishmael without being subjected to any lists:

- Ishmael is a restless soul.
- He is evidently not a rich man.
- He has no family ties to hold him to a particular place.
- He is ironic, about himself and others.

The combination of melancholy and his 'hypos' suggests a temperament we might nowadays call manic-depressive. And the urgency of his tone suggests a trenchant mind.

The economy of means employed to convey all this biographical data so rapidly, and without employing any type of catalogue, deserves study. This is writing of a high standard, as can be seen by the swiftness with which it relocates us from our daily reality into the fictional one.

Now contrast this with a very different opening:

It is a truth universally acknowledged, that a single man in possession of a good fortune, must be in want of a wife.

now you do it

Inciting incidents

Stories often begin with an 'inciting incident' – for example, Pip is accosted by Magwitch in the marshes at the beginning of *Great Expectations* and from this meeting, the story develops. Write a list of six of your own ideas for inciting incidents.

This is the famous first sentence of Jane Austen's *Pride and Prejudice*. We might consider the differences. Firstly this is not first-person, but third-person. This voice is distanced from the fray it is about to describe; it seems detached and ironic. It is obviously the omniscient narrator of the classic realist novel, and the choice of language reflects that dispassionate, God-like orientation. 'It is a truth universally acknowledged' really means that you and I, dear reader, know how human beings prefer to justify their actions by invoking universal principles, when what is really in play is the most individual of motivations. There is just as much of a conspiracy of tone here as there is in *Moby Dick*, but where one is urgent, demotic, street-wise, the other is Olympian in its stately knowingness. Here we see the contrast between the first- and third-person narrative voice at its most extreme. Let us look at another famous opening (that of Dickens' *Great Expectations*) and see what skills the writer is employing:

My father's family name being Pirrip, and my christian name Philip, my infant tongue could make of both names nothing longer or more explicit than Pip. So I called myself Pip, and came to be called Pip.

I give Pirrip as my father's family name, on the authority of his tombstone and my sister – Mrs. Joe Gargery, who married the blacksmith. As I never saw my father or my mother, and never saw any likeness of either of them (for their days were long before the days of photographs), my first fancies regarding what they were like, were unreasonably derived from their tombstones. The shape of the letters on my father's, gave me an odd idea that he was a square, stout, dark man, with curly black hair.

From the character and turn of the inscription, 'Also Georgiana Wife of the Above,' I drew a childish conclusion that my mother was freckled and sickly. To five little stone lozenges, each about a foot and a half long, which were sacred to the memory of five little brothers of mine – who gave up trying to get a living exceedingly early in that universal struggle – I am indebted for a belief I religiously entertained that they had all been born on their back with their hands in their trousers-pockets, and had never taken them out in this state of existence.

This is brilliant in conveying the vividness and not necessarily rational movements of a child's mind; the way that an image is immediately transformed into a representative reality. But this is not a child's language, something indicated by the employment of the give-away adjective 'childish'.

We are supplied with a great deal of information obliquely. If Pip's parents lived before the possibilities of photography then they must have died before the 1840s, when photography first started to become popular. If Pip can talk of his brothers giving up trying to get a living in that 'universal struggle', then we should pick up an echo. The phrase 'universal struggle for existence' was used in Chapter Three of Charles Darwin's *Origin of Species*, published in 1859. *Great Expectations* began serial publication in 1860. This is childhood recollected with a very adult syntax and vocabulary. Compare it with another novel's opening:

Once upon a time and a very good time it was there was a moocow coming down along the road and this moocow that was coming down along the road met a nicens little boy named baby tuckoo....

now you do it

The narrative voice

The most radical way to utterly change the nature of a piece of fiction, even if the plot remains exactly the same, is to change the voice. Try writing a story in first-person then changing the pronouns and verbs to make it third-person. The results can be fresh and interesting.

must know

An announcement

The tone of the opening announces a world. The voice we hear on the page, and the type of voice (first-person; third-person) tell us whose company we will be keeping. The opening of any piece of fiction should never be hesitant.

What the beginning of James Joyce's *Portrait of the Artist As A Young Man* does is to try to situate us linguistically inside the mind of the child. In fact, all five chapters of that pioneering work of what we call the Modern Movement reflect stylistically the stages of Stephen Dedalus's mind as he grows through his Catholic childhood and education to adulthood and apostasy, an apostasy adopted in the name of art. What is being subverted here is the knowing, authorial tone that can look back upon childhood and re-create it from a position of linguistic and stylistic superiority.

What all four of these openings show us is how a skilled writer announces a world, a consciousness, a textual identity, which lets the reader know that we have crossed the line between the world and the book. The book, while we are inside it, is the world. Every choice of vocabulary, syntax, intonation, even punctuation, will either make that world convincing or fail to do so.

Coleridge spoke of the 'willing suspension of disbelief' that we must volunteer as readers or spectators if we are to enter the world of a work of art. Such a suspension can only be earned by the accomplishment of the writing. We learn how to do this by studying the serious achievements of those who have gone before.

The beginning, then, is the announcement of a new world, the world of the book or story. It should make its announcement as economically and potently as possible. Many publishers only read the first page of a manuscript. They know by then whether or not they have been invited into a convincing world.

The meaning of character

Let us keep reminding ourselves what fiction is.

Fiction is the exploration of reality in words by means of the invention and portrayal of character. It can be many other things too, but it will not be fiction without this pervasive sense of the reality of character.

So why do we have to say both invention and portrayal? A novel or story can be based entirely on historical characters, but unless there is a degree of invention, if only in conveying the psychology of these characters, then it will be some sort of historical writing, not fiction. It can be obsessed with place, but unless convincing characters appear convincingly within that place, it will be classified as travel writing, or geography, or topography. Fiction can and often does have a large documentary element; but it cannot afford to be entirely documentary, or it loses its 'fictiveness'.

We cannot look for long at fiction of any sort without discussing character. Fiction explores its realities through the probing and exposition of character. Let us think of what we call a historical novel. As the term implies, this is based upon certain characters who have had a historical existence; we can check them out. Documentary evidence of some sort is available. But why should anyone want to read a fictionalized account? Why not simply stick with the historical deposits? Why not read the biographies and letters of Wilfred Owen and Siegfried Sassoon, rather than reading Pat Barker's *Regeneration*? The answer to that can only be found in the way fiction allows for the exposition, critique and development of character. Barker does

now you do it

Studying character

Every minute of the day can count as a character study for the attentive writer. The way someone speaks, combs their hair, puts on a hat, smoothes down a skirt, speaks of a friend. Studying the human gestures all around you is as much genuine research as travelling to Morocco to observe the local dances there. Write short pieces describing the distinctive gestures of ten people you know as if you are introducing them in a story.

not 'invent' either Owen or Sassoon, but in a sense she re-invents them by the employment of her fictional skill. Fiction creates a space that allows us to probe character, emotion and experience.

What do we mean by character?

The word 'character' still carries its original sense of a distinctive sign on either body or soul. This notion of a mark or an emblem that shows the distinctiveness of that which it marks survives in the usage of 'character' to mean individual letters in an alphabet. So character is distinctiveness, the signature of a person in word and deed, or in silence and inaction. Let us list some of the salient features of character that most of us would recognize:

- Appearance
- Gesture
- Speech/silence
- Action/inaction
- Mode of interaction with others
- Dutifulness/waywardness
- Attentiveness to others/disregard of others
- Boldness/timorousness
- Talent/inability

These give us a rough summary of the qualities which, taken together, make up someone's 'character'. It is by a selective use of certain of these attributes that a writer *characterizes* a person in a book. The way in which the figure enters the *mise-en-scène* of the fiction will often tell us a great deal about his or her character. The better the writer, the more effective will be the conveyance of identity and character. Every gesture, every word, must contribute potently to the picture we are forming of the new arrival.

In terms of narrative technique, there are usually two forms of character portrayal: character by report and character by exposition; in other words, telling or showing. The first can be performed either by the author or by other characters in the text. The second is conveyed by the words, deeds and thoughts of the actual character.

The writer can either tell the reader what someone in the work is like, even if the telling has to come through the ventriloquism of a textual character, or show it, by letting the character speak and act for him/herself.

Telling versus showing

Character is conveyed either by telling or showing.

Telling: the character is described either by the author or another character.

Showing: the character describes him/herself to us by thought, word or deed.

This distinction between telling and showing will recur throughout this book. When Joseph Heller tells us in the first line of *Catch-22* that the first time Yossarian saw the army chaplain, he fell madly in love with him, he is giving us a great deal of information in a short space. He is certainly not telling us that Yossarian is gay, for he isn't. He is telling us that he is impulsive, wayward, almost dementedly wishful. He is telling us that he is in the army.

Within pages we will discover that the army is at war during the Second World War. And he is announcing, as clearly as the opening page of *Alice in Wonderland*, that we are about to enter a weird and unexpected world. Alice's intelligence is more

now you do it

Working from art

Choose three portraits by well-known artists. Examples could be Rembrandt's portrait of his wife Saskia, Holbein's *The Ambassadors*, or one of Lucian Freud's nude women. Write a short, first-person piece for each character trying to capture what you think their voice would be like.

conservative than the reality that is soon surrounding her:

...suddenly a white rabbit with pink eyes ran close by her. There was nothing so very remarkable in that; nor did Alice think it so very much out of the way to hear the Rabbit say to itself, 'Oh dear! Oh dear! I shall be too late!'

We are learning effortlessly about Alice's character here. She is not easily flustered, and faced with all the surreal events that are about to confront her, she tends to exhibit an unremitting practicality and good sense.

In fact she is far more adult than any of the adults in Wonderland. But Lewis Carroll does not have to tell us this. He lets Alice show us herself, by her own thoughts, words and deeds. This is showing, not telling.

It is interesting how we often use the phrase 'betray' in relation to characterization. We say how a person's actions betray their true intent. Someone's slip of the tongue betrays their true feelings. This is an old notion, but one that has gained a modern terminology as a result of the work of Sigmund Freud. Now we often talk about unconscious motivations or desires, and such terminology conveys the notion that our outward appearance is as much a disguise as a free expression.

Our true motivations are often as opaque to ourselves as they are to others. Our true identity lies underneath the apparent one. Much modern fiction is engaged in enquiring into this seeming contradiction, and the monstrosities of behaviour it can engender.

Albert Camus' novel *The Outsider* finds its radicalism in Meursault's refusal of conventional emotion. His mother dies, and he doesn't seem to care much. He kills a man on a beach and refuses to repent, since the act meant nothing to him. Such narratives have a long lineage in modern fiction.

Dostoyevsky's *Notes from Underground* is premised entirely on the deliberated disaffection of its protagonist. This is not someone who has tragically slipped out of social life; this is someone who has casually renounced it as being of no significance. In a great deal of modern writing, character is portrayed as a refusal of social requirement; it can come across as steadfast negativity. It is a writing of self-conscious alienation.

Language and character

One of the means for the conveyance of character in fiction is the character's own language. Think of the way we are brought vividly into the presence of Tom Sawyer or Huckleberry Finn by the words Mark Twain puts into their mouths. A whole world is conjured by a couple of expressions. We've already seen the same thing in the opening lines of *Moby Dick*. And, continuing the American tradition, Saul Bellow created many characters whose worlds appear to us first through the distinctiveness of their language. *Herzog* begins memorably:

If I am out of my mind, it's all right with me, thought Moses Herzog.

This last sentence introduces us to a type of voicing of fiction which is neither first-person, like Melville,

now you do it

Dialogue

Every time a character speaks or thinks in fiction, that person's identity is being expressed. The choice of words, and their shaping into sentences, should convey this fact. List some of the differences in vocabulary and syntax that you might expect from an urban teenager, a grandmother living in remote countryside, a City banker and an eight-year-old child. Write a dialogue between two of them.

nor third-person, like Jane Austen. This is known as the free indirect style. The author retains the all-knowing, or omniscient, stance of the third-person, but slips so far inside the consciousness of the character that it is as if we inhabit that character's mind.

You'll find more about this useful technique on page 23.

In all this it should be remembered that character is not univocal or unequivocal, and the best writers convey this. If a character is entirely univocal, ie speaking in a single voice, then we often call that character either 'flat' or a caricature. In both cases we are making a contrast with those 'rounded characters' who convey a genuine sense of their own reality.

Character is diverse, variegated, even polarized. It is not a homogenized entity. And character can be altered, distorted, broken or crystallized by the effect of action upon it. Nevertheless, it must remain sufficiently coherent to be evidently *this* character. Pip goes through many changes in the course of *Great Expectations*, but he is still identifiably Pip at the end. His character is large enough to permit development.

Narrative voice

The manner of the telling alters the tale. For example, right at the beginning of *Great Expectations* we know that we are in the presence of Pip, an older Pip than the Pip being presented to us in that graveyard. Dickens is here exploiting the potentialities of the first-person narrative. Let's have a look at what the different types of narrative voice are.

First-person narrative

The distinctive characteristics of first-person are:
- Intimacy
- Confidentiality
- Bias
- Impossibility of knowing everything

Let us start with this last quality first. If I am the all-knowing or omniscient narrator then I can tell you that while Dick slept in London, his wife Judy in France was making love to a man she only met earlier that day. This is only possible for the omniscient narrator. Dick cannot know this, unless he is told. His circumscribed consciousness means that if he comes by any information, then it must be by credible means. Judy could phone him, wake him up, and let him know, to punish him in some way. But there cannot simply be a neutral way of knowing these things, in the way that there is for the omniscient narrator.

Now we go back to the beginning of the list.

Intimacy

I feel as though something is gnawing away inside me like a hungry rat in an empty cupboard.

We share Dick's feelings, and this entails sharing his ignorance too. Because he cannot know something, we cannot know it either. We are experiencing the plot with him, encountering other characters as he does, sharing the hidden secrets of his diaries, his letters, his memories, his joys and fears.

Confidentiality

I have decided to tell no one about this.

Dick can tell us this, and we don't feel we have to object, 'But you just told me.' As a reader we are as close to Dick as his own heartbeat. We take it for granted that we are let in from the beginning. It is hard to imagine a first-person narrative that does not permit such privileged entry. That is the function of this voicing. The first-person mode of fiction is the voicing of circumscribed consciousness. We occupy the same circle of self as the protagonist. Reality bears down upon us from all the same directions.

must know

Choosing the voice

The voicing of a text is one of the writer's resources. It is important to make the right choice since this will facilitate the writing; the wrong choice will hinder it. A tale of obsession often needs to be told from the inside, using the first-person, whereas a satirical account of a group of people might need the distancing possibilities of the third-person. The free-indirect style allows for both possibilities.

Bias

I know she didn't have to do that. This wasn't justice she was seeking, but revenge.

No consciousness embedded in a first-person text is ever neutral. Only the god-like narrator can lay claim to such neutrality. So we share the bias – emotional, amatory, intellectual, moral – of the narrator in whose narrative we have been enmeshed. If we can disengage entirely from a first-person narrative then the author has lost us. Bias is a seeming limitation which in the hands of a skilful writer is exploited so it becomes a bonus.

Third-person narrative

All of the above qualities are either reversed or put into suspension when we use the third-person voicing.

Dick was trapped inside his own pain; he could no longer make out the borders of his own life, or where those borders separated from the lives of others.

Dick may be trapped but we are no longer trapped with him in one consciousness. We do not have to share the emotions, difficulties or joys of the protagonist. There is now no limit to the amount of knowledge we are permitted regarding other characters and their doings. This is not to say we cannot be sympathetic. But the sympathy, the sharing of a reality, is by no means obligatory.

At the beginning of *The Shipping News,* Annie Proulx describes Quoyle, the poor benighted character whose astounding misfortunes and ultimate redemption form the core of her novel. It would feel very different if the narrative were to be voiced by Quoyle himself. Our ability to stand outside Quoyle and watch the terrible repression of his feelings is part of the power of Proulx's prose.

The third-person narrator can be everywhere at once, in whatever mind, exploring his or her emotions at will. Its advantage then is its panoramic scope. Its disadvantage, if not used intelligently, is a chilling distance and detachment.

now you do it

Interviewing

Some writers find it helpful to 'interview' characters they invent. Pretend you are a journalist, and ask them about their family background, work, interests, relationships, religious beliefs, politics, favourite leisure pursuits and so forth. Write out the responses you imagine your character would give. It's a useful way of catching the voice.

The free indirect style

There is a type of voicing that steers a midway between these two alternatives. It is called the free indirect style, and it has become a greatly favoured resource of the modern writer. The voice slides from third- to first-person, without the need for inverted commas. In other words, the text itself, for the elected period, inhabits the chosen consciousness:

Dick stood at the bus-stop in the rain. He stared up at the black sky. It didn't look as though there was much chance of any let-up in the weather. For the rain it raineth every day. Why, he thought. Why do I have to stand here morning after morning with wet feet and a damp head, going to work in a place I don't like, amongst people I don't much care for, so I can bring back enough money to stay alive for one more day and then start all over again the next...

Once we have entered Dick's monologue, it can continue for as long as the fiction needs it. Then we can return to the third-person. In this manner, the free indirect style combines the benefits of the first-person and the third.

now you do it

Ten commandments

Write your own ten commandments for writers and order them in terms of importance. They could include strong characterization, vivid dialogue, honest observation, lively description, well-paced plotting, elegant prose, powerful imagery, universal themes... Choose your personal top ten and prioritize them.

A modern American writer such as David Foster Wallace exploits this resource to exhilarating effect in books such as *Brief Interviews With Hideous Men*; though if we look carefully we will see that it has been part of the fiction writer's repertoire for centuries.

A person's character is the signature they leave in the spaces they inhabit. We sign ourselves in words, deeds, facial expression, writing, work - whatever takes up our days. Even if we spend all day long sitting by the railway track playing a beaten-up old guitar, that is still a signature. Put enough of these signatures together and we start to perceive someone's character. But the way in which that character is voiced - by themselves or someone else - is crucial. So characterization and voicing are closely related subjects.

Think how often we might say about someone: but you need to hear him tell the story himself. Why? Because something of the character of the anecdote has been lost by changing the voicing.

We could not really take a character like Holden Caulfield in *The Catcher in the Rye* and convey him as fully in the third-person. He needs to speak to us directly, as Huckleberry Finn does; we need to hear these voices to savour the piquancy of the characters. If you doubt this intimate relationship between character and voice, think how often you can hear a voice on the telephone and put a name to it before the person has identified themselves.

Writing is still referred to sometimes as composition, and it is a useful term with which to think about characterization. If we are composing a picture, we decide upon what is to be included in the frame, what excluded; how the different objects will stand in relation to one another; and from what angle we should view the whole. This is also the situation in writing about character.

- How do people normally present themselves?
- What are the most notable things about them?
- What distinguishes them from others in a room, and what makes them disappear into a crowd?
- Do I, as a writer, creep up on them, overhear them, see them arrive with others or alone?

If we first glimpse someone in fiction laughing and joking at a party, then that gives a very different impression from first seeing the same person alone at midnight, writing by lamplight.

Our first impression can, of course, be used to effect a contrast with the true character. We first see him at that party, but later we see him alone beneath the lamplight, and come to feel that his real identity lies in the second frame rather than the first. Or perhaps both aspects of him are equally true. After all, very few of us have an entirely singular identity. Convincing characters are normally a little complicated, in fiction as in life.

want to know more?

- **As you will learn in chapter 2, all the best plots are character-led.**
- **See chapter 3 for advice on the way the setting can illuminate fictional characters.**
- **Go through your bookshelves and pick out the novels with a very distinctive central character. Think about how the author created that character. Identify the narrative voice and consider how the story would have to change if any other voice had been used.**
- **Read any Dickens novel and note how he conjures up a character in very few words.**
- **There's a glossary of fictional terms on pages 183–89.**

2 Plot

Plot is the way that history happens in fiction, whether that 'history' takes place in the past, the present or the future. Plot is what goes on between our characters and beyond, even if this 'going on' is now taking place inside a human mind or memory.
In modern fiction, the plot must ultimately seem like the expected outcome of the situation and the characterization; it must finally be made to feel 'natural'.

Plot

How can you create an effective plot that makes readers want to keep reading what you have written? In this chapter we'll have a look at what a good plot requires.

must know

Creating pace

What creates pace in writing? The intelligent sequencing of information. This is really what plotting is: the release of information in a controlled sequence that provides sufficient knowledge now to secure our attention, but not so much that we feel we have already had enough. Suspense is another way of saying that we want to know more. That is the motivation which turns the page.

Action

Action of any sort requires a reversal of fortune or a change of circumstance. Otherwise one simply has 'development'. Development uninterrupted by any checks or obstacles might make for a tranquil life, but it makes for very dull fiction. One ends up with something like this:

James and Jenny were both very happy. They lived in Surrey, and were devoted to one another. They had three beautiful and contented children, all of whom grew up to be happy and contented in their turn. After a long and fulfilling life...

You get the picture. It might be a pleasant plan for a life, but it's hardly what you would wish to read in a work of fiction. Development here is uninterrupted by any reversal of fortune.

Now imagine the difference in the passage above if it was suddenly to be sliced across by the words, 'But then one dreadful day...' We show an interest immediately. The fact is that fiction is fascinated by darkness and misfortune, and 'plot' is usually the negotiation of this by those whom the darkness, however temporarily, enshrouds. What might horrify us in life tends to magnetize us in writing.

This is never more apparent than in the work of

Dickens. His good characters can sometimes risk anaemia; his evil ones are always vivid: Bill Sykes; Uriah Heep; Magwitch in the graveyard. They enter the imagination and will not come out. And what the bad characters do in a Dickens plot is to impede the otherwise tranquil 'development' of the lives of the good.

The machinery that ultimately contains all these goings-on is called the plot. Here the writer needs to make an important distinction: plot is not so much what happens as the *presentation* of what happens. It is not the story – not how A was followed by B then followed by C. It is the sequencing of this information, the granting and withholding of knowledge about events, that makes for effective plotting. This can be seen very simply. Here is the first sentence of a detective story:

Mrs Margaret Fell shot Jonathan Hoyle in the chest with a revolver when she discovered that it wasn't only her duvet he'd been sharing.

That's the first sentence of the detective story, but also the last. Of course, had we simply been presented with Hoyle's body lying on a carpet somewhere, then immediately the chase is on. We have been presented with the riddle; now we wish to solve it. This seems straightforward enough in a genre such as the detective story, but the same principle of selective revelation in fact applies to all types of fiction, or even all types of writing. If the Dramatis Personae at the beginning of Sophocles' play *Oedipus Rex* said: 'Oedipus: King of Thebes, Husband and Son of Jocasta, Killer of his father Laius', then the play ends before it begins.

now you do it

Plot a detective story

Whether you are interested in writing in this genre or not, it can be a useful exercise to plan a detective plot. Try the following. Your character comes home from an ordinary day at work to find a dead body in the house. He/she doesn't know the corpse in question, but has a secret that makes them unwilling to involve the police. Jot down your own notes about how this story could develop.

So plot is not chronology; in fact it is frequently at variance with chronology. Plot tends to oscillate between the present and the past, revealing at any one time only segments of the final arc of revelations. Good plotting consists of choosing the right amount of information to lay before the reader at any one time. It is for this reason that plotting is inseparable from characterization.

The function of plot in fiction is often to express character; character is the psychological verification of the movements of plot. Henry James summarized the situation over a century ago: 'What is character but the determination of incident? What is incident but the illustration of character?'

We have now used the word psychology and should explore its implications for a moment. If we go back to our ancient distinction between fable, fiction and history, where fiction is the middle category, we can see something interesting:

Fable/Fiction/History

Looking at history, I can give an account of the battles of the Great War without exploring the psychology of any of the combatants; I am permitted to leave the psychology out of account. Looking at fable, I can also tell you the story of Red Riding Hood without mentioning in any way the little girl's psychology. This is of no account. Only the events concerning the grandmother, the wolf, the woodcutter, and their ultimate resolution matter.

But this cannot be the case with modern fiction. It is precisely the psychological depth and resonance that Pat Barker brings to her writing in *Regeneration* that makes us want to read it. And when a modern writer returns to legendary matter, as Margaret Atwood does in *The Penelopiad*, it is the new-found psychology that will provide the revelation. This is precisely why we want to read the book.

If plot separates itself sufficiently from psychology, we say that it is mechanical. We are seeing too much external manipulation of events, and too little internal development, or psychology. Devices such as coincidence can be employed to lead to too facile a redemption of difficulties, although David Mitchell in *Ghostwritten* uses coincidence and serendipity to link a collection of otherwise diverse stories. A wrong number dialled on a telephone, a chance meeting on a street, can change lives irrevocably. The point is that Mitchell is not using such devices as a default setting. He is not employing them unconsciously or sentimentally; he is consciously engaging them as tactical ploys. We will return to this theme on pages 132–37 in a section on Coincidence.

One way of putting this is to say that two principles in life and logic must be satisfactorily combined in the balance between plotting and characterization. We can call them Causality and Contingency.

A definition

Causality: what must happen, the ultimate explanation for everything; the final meaning of the plot.

Contingency: what might happen but doesn't have to. The realm of freedom. The element that constantly brings the plot into question. The element that, in the writing of a book, sometimes ends up changing the plot in a manner the writer didn't originally intend.

We could make a crude summary of the situation thus. Excessive causality means predictable characters and too many coincidences. Excessive contingency means that the narrative disintegrates into incoherence.

now you do it

Write an age-old story

Choose one of the age-old plots listed on this page and write a story based on it, but give it a realistic modern setting. For example, the monster could be an unreasonable employer, an ASBO kid on the block, or even a computer that crashes frequently.

The plot is what must finally happen. We know this both as readers and writers. It is the mechanism of causality. But psychology is the realm of contingency. Things here can always be otherwise. Someone might 'change their mind'. One of the reasons many publishers turned down Frederick Forsyth's *Day of the Jackal* was that the causality was too well-known. The plot concerned an attempt to assassinate President de Gaulle but everyone knew that de Gaulle did not get assassinated. In fact, this reaction underestimated the force of contingency in fiction. The motivations and adventures of the would-be assassin could be sufficiently compelling in themselves. After all, we already know what happened in the Great War, and we know that Wilfred Owen died while Siegfried Sassoon survived, but we still want to read *Regeneration*.

Some age-old plots

It has frequently been argued that there are a fixed number of archetypal plots: that is to say, certain motifs that tend to recur in one form or another throughout world literature. Here are a number of the most identifiable ones:

- The battle with the monster.
- The quest.
- The voyage and the return home.
- The hero hidden as the monster.
- The divided self.
- The engagement with the dark power.
- The fatal flaw.
- The journey from rags to riches.
- The voyage to the underworld.

What tends to happen in modern writing is that we move from mythology to psychology. Those archetypal plots that were explored as actual journeys, magical landscapes, identifiable topographies, in legend or classical drama or epic, become internalized in modern fiction. This means that they discover for themselves a psychological dimension which was not there before.

The voyage to the underworld is more likely to be an account of mental disintegration or addiction than an actual itinerary, such as Dante's in *The Divine Comedy* or Virgil's in the *Aeneid*. It might now be Irvine Welsh's *Trainspotting*, or even an allegory of alienation like Kafka's story *Metamorphosis*. Or it could be Arthur Clennam's descent to the Marshalsea Prison in Dickens's novel, *Little Dorrit*.

In its modern form, the hero hidden as the monster is more likely to be the Elephant Man, or an undiagnosed schizophrenic, than the actual feral creature of Beauty and the Beast.

Modern writers often subvert the genres they work in. They deliberately disappoint expectations. When Joyce in *Ulysses* presents us with our modern hero he is an anti-hero, not heroic in the old sense at all. There is an ironic distance between the heroic patterning of the book through Homeric myth, and the dailiness of life in Dublin in 1904.

Samuel Beckett carried on where Joyce left off. Although it is a play, *Waiting for Godot* exemplifies many of the same characteristics as Joyce's fiction. It has been described as a play in which nothing happens, twice. Its radicalism lay in its refusal of any easy satisfaction. Two tramps stand in the road. The only reason for their being there is to meet Godot,

must know

Looking inwards

The movement of plotting in modern fiction has often been a shift inwards. The dramas that Leopold Bloom lives through in James Joyce's *Ulysses* are psychological and sexual, rather than the mighty struggles out on the open seas that his fictional progenitor Odysseus endured. This is another way of saying that we live in the age of psychology. We cannot simply present characters doing a multitude of things: the reader wants to know why they are doing them. We are as intrigued by the 'why' as the 'how'.

but Godot never arrives. And they are thrown back upon their own resources, the resources of language, mockery, humour and the forensic examination of their own despair. The plot here is about the disappearance of 'plot' in any traditional sense.

Alienation

This raises a question about the role of alienation in modern writing. Alienation points to a disconnection at the heart of things. In classic realist fiction, alienation is explained, and then usually resolved; in modern fiction it is just as likely to be presupposed, and ultimately left in place. It is simply in the nature of things. How does this affect plotting? As often as not, it will be by introducing the fragmentary as a condition of life.

In good modern writing, it is very seldom that everything gets resolved. How could it? It is one of the faults of Dickens that the endings of his novels over-resolve. Everyone with any virtue must be paired off and provided for. Anyone tainted by evil must be disposed of, either in this life or the next. This is the sort of

Fragmentation

Hemingway's stories in the two 1920s collections *In Our Time* and *Men Without Women* exploit fragmentation by using montage effects borrowed from cinema. Short passages of text alternate one with another, and give a sense of the rapidity and unexpectedness, the unjoined-up quality, of modern existence. Here, the fictive possibilities of redemption, sometimes known as poetic justice, are withdrawn. Life's actual inconsequence and fatal lack of coherence are presented in its place. Any grand words meant to comfort tend to be emptied of their comfort. This alienated stance is characteristic of much modern writing.

ending described by Henry James as 'a distribution at the last of prizes, pensions, husbands, wives, babies, millions, appended paragraphs, and cheerful remarks.' It does not ring true to us.

Far truer seems that element of fragmentation and irresolution used so effectively by writers like Joyce or Hemingway.

Obviously this is also a matter of the type of writing, or its genre. If we are reading a detective story, for instance, then we are entitled to expect certain things of the plot: a crime, an investigative intelligence, a series of confusions and an ultimate resolution that will fit together all that was previously broken apart, so that the whole makes sense. That is what we might call a genre requirement. But even here a modern writer such as Ian Rankin does not expect to resolve things with the universal finality of a Sherlock Holmes story. When all the causality has worked itself through, there is still a lot of contingency to ponder.

Moving towards resolution

So what are the motors that move a work of fiction on from its beginning? The answer to that question is plot and characterization, which is to say the shape of the work and its different voicings. The philosopher Kierkegaard once remarked that we write biographies backwards, but have to live our lives forwards. It is the balance between plot and character, between causality and contingency, that makes the writing read as if it had been written forwards, even if it had to be plotted in the other direction. Dickens, in so fiercely plotting his redemptive endings, is seen to have forfeited verisimilitude. He has abandoned contingency too readily, in favour of a contrived causality.

What a modern writer of fiction cannot afford to be is naïve. Resolutions cannot be casually effected by coincidence, because such a reliance on underlying synchronicities might seem like the return of magic to a disenchanted world. Fiction's

must know

Borrowing plots

There are no new plots, so there's not much point trying to invent one. Many writers don't bother inventing plots at all: they simply borrow them. Such borrowings should always lead to new insights. Think of the way Angela Carter took traditional tales and turned them around by seeing them from a different sexual angle. Perhaps the girl in the story does not need to kill the male wolf after all. She might enjoy becoming vulpine herself. Why not try retelling a traditional tale and giving it a modern setting and your own distinctive style?

plot represents its map of possibilities. It negotiates the border between freedom and control.

All plotting has to end in a revelation of some sort. This is what the word *dénoument* actually means: it is the French for unknotting. In other words, the various strands of the story have been so entangled that we could not make them all out before. Now at last we see the relationship between contingency and causality, between choice and fate. We finally grasp the plot.

All plots imply a primary disturbance, a movement from stasis, a wrenching of things from the places they had previously occupied, and the ultimate resolution carries the sense of a restoration of order, which is to say a restoration of (relative) stasis. This might be after catastrophe and catharsis have done their worst, but a resolution is still implied.

When modern writers play around with these conventions they know that they still form the background to such subversions. So Joyce ends *Finnegans Wake* halfway through the sentence that started it, and Thomas Pynchon in *The Crying of Lot 49* writes the whole book so that the final words recapitulate the title. We must read the entire text to arrive at the meaning of the book's first words.

A plot is a journey, even if it is only undertaken inside a character's head: we are still engaged in intellectual movement, via the words. In some of the works of Samuel Beckett a character is immobile in a room, in a chair or on a bed, but we still move through the landscape of the plot with them mentally. They recall their past (so we return there); they recall lost loves (so we imagine these); they

Hooking the reader

How can you make the reader pick up your work, read the first page and then keep on reading? They need to be entertained, absorbed, transported to the world you have created. Try to think of plot ideas that would have the following effects on your readers:

Educated
Intrigued
Saddened
Frightened
Angered
Reassured
Changed

want to know more?

- **See chapter 7 for more on irony and chapter 8 for an analysis of how humour works in fiction.**
- **Compare the way plot works in a film with the way it works in a novel. Read Robert McKee's famous book *Story* for an analysis of the cinematic formula.**
- **Kurt Vonnegut said that you can draw all plots as a graph of the leading characters' fortunes. Try doing this with some of your favourite books.**
- **Keep a cuttings file of articles that interest you from newspapers or magazines. Keep adding to it and next time you are looking for an idea for a new story, sort through your cuttings, filing them loosely by subject. You're bound to find ideas.**

recollect old joys, old fears, old sufferings (so these too are paraded before our reading eyes).

Plot is inescapable. In writing it is always presented through words, since words represent the full extent of the fiction writer's resources. In this sense, then, the words themselves are the plot. This means that all of the resources of language must be employed to achieve the greatest effects in language. With each use of irony or humour a fracture opens up in the text, a dissonant space which we must cross: each of these constitutes another tiny journey. Jokes too are a part of the plot.

3 Setting

All books are set inside their own covers, but given that, the writer can take us to any place or any time. The setting in time and place is an aspect of plot; and plot is the expression of characterization. All our categories meet and intermingle; that is the nature of fiction. But if you are travelling to a distant place, or a distant time, then you must be sure that you can present us with the details that are going to evoke that place or time with some confidence. If you falter, it will not be merely 'setting' that looks thin, but character and plot too.

Setting

City or country? At home or abroad? All these decisions will depend on the type of story you want to tell and the way you want to tell it.

now you do it

Two sentences

A place and a time can be evoked with great economy by a few striking details. Practise conveying the feel of a place in a couple of sentences: this is often all that fiction needs.

Time and place

At the beginning of Jill Dawson's *Wild Boy* we are simply given these words:

Thermidor 16/ Year Eight in our Glorious Republic.

The first words of *Wuthering Heights* are:

1801 – I have just returned from a visit to my landlord – the solitary neighbour that I shall be troubled with. This is certainly a beautiful country! In all England, I do not believe that I could have fixed on a situation so completely removed from the stir of society.

We live after Einstein, and this means that we know that time and place can never be meaningfully separated. To every 'where' there is a 'when'. To pretend otherwise is a deception. Even our fantasies are rooted in time.

Remember the Wizard of Oz? He turned out to be just a man after all, but his manipulation of the machinery ties him to a particular state of technology. What was once modern is now dated. In writing, even the future soon fades into the past.

The ultimate setting of all writing is words on a page. No writer can afford to forget this, since it is this that finally will dictate either success or failure. Most contemporary fiction is set in the present. It is written out of the lived experience of the writer. The advantage of this to the writer is evident: you do not have to research this, since you are researching it by getting up each morning. Yet this very dailiness can also be a disadvantage, for it might exclude the marvellous – though on pages 48–52 we will discuss defamiliarization, the purpose of which is to render the ordinary as marvellous as possible.

By choosing settings in a different place and time from where we live, we provide ourselves with resources which our own location might not offer. There is an exoticism to alternative geographical and temporal locations, which is both a temptation and a danger.

Let us go back to Jill Dawson's *Wild Boy*. She has based this novel on the Wild Boy of Aveyron, an actual child found living wild in France in the 18th century. He had already been the subject of a film by the French director François Truffaut. As those opening words make plain, we are still in the throes of post-revolutionary France. One of the deeds of the *citoyens* was to re-invent the calendar, to show that the old age had gone for ever. But more information is provided in the use of the word 'our'. If the person writing this date in this manner is prepared to talk of 'our glorious republic', then we know he is for the revolution, not against it.

And this turns out to be the case. Doctor Itard is glad to see the back of the *ancien régime*. He is a modern rational man, a man of the Enlightenment, and it falls to him to attempt to induct the young savage into the language and customs of society. Already the setting provides us with a world; settings always do. We are living at a different time and in a

now you do it

Character in setting

Introduce a character by describing an element of the setting in which they are found. 'Show' rather than 'tell'. Always put your character into a situation and let them crawl out rather than attacking character description head on.

now you do it

Getting involved

You need to become involved in a time and place, intellectually engaged with it, if you are to convey it effectively in fiction. Choose a historical period with which you are familiar and describe a character eating a meal, letting the way they eat inform readers about both their character and their era.

different culture. This offers excitement, but it does give the writer a lot of work to do. The further the setting is from the writer's actual conditions of life, the more research is required.

There is enough documentary evidence to provide Dawson with the outline of her story, but also enough gaps in that story to provoke the fictionalization. Who was this boy? How did he come to be living wild? What had caused the gash around his throat – an animal or a human being? Would it still be possible to teach him language now that he had spent so many years without it? Fiction enters the gaps that history has left behind, and this is one of the things historical writing does, both here and in *Regeneration*.

The characters in the novel start to assert their own identities. Itard might be for the Revolution. Others are not. Character variation and dynamism begin to separate the elements of an 'overall situation' into a variegated plot. Very quickly the setting in space and time has become the location for the fictionalization. Because of the remarkable skill of the writing, we quickly forget the strangeness of being transported back two centuries in time, to another culture in which people spoke another language. The setting has become instead an invitation to our curiosity.

The date of *Wuthering Heights* on the first page of the book is important, because most of the narrative that follows will be about events before that date. By the time Lockwood, our narrator, arrives on the scene, some of the most important characters are already dead. This is why we have to emphasize that setting is always location in both time and place.

But setting is also a matter of emotion and psychology. The fact is that *Wuthering Heights* might be set on the Yorkshire Moors, and the weather is sufficiently dramatic that it almost kills Lockwood on one occasion, but it is set equally inside the passionate temperaments of Heathcliff and Cathy; their internal meteorology is as striking and unfathomable as the commotion of the northern weather outside. We are exploring landscapes both internal and external; and much of the book is about the exploration of memory. The events recounted are being recalled, and one way to read the ghost-scene is as an acknowledgment that memory traces in a particular world can be as potent as the living themselves.

must know

Learn to cut

In writing we often do a lot of research about places which doesn't make it through to the final text. Why? Because it is boring. We had to do it all the same, to find out all we needed to know about this part of our setting, but we need to be gracious. Writers must endure their research; this doesn't mean that readers always have to suffer through it too. Learn how to cut the inessential.

Economy of means

Setting, like any other fictional device, requires its own economy of means. Whatever is being employed, either in the way of topographic detail or period data, needs to function in the text. We need to ask continually, what is it for? How does it enrich this particular narrative?

- Where are we?
- When are we?
- What are we?

Think how much the answers to these questions are historically and culturally conditioned in any piece of writing. All fiction is answering all three questions on every page. Narrative always implies location in both time and place. Even in Samuel Beckett's accounts of the lives of those without

must know

Vivid settings

***Treasure Island. Moby Dick. Catch-22.* We remember the vivid settings of all these works of fiction. On boats. On islands. Searching for treasure or for whales. Fighting a very dangerous war and, when not nearly being killed, searching for sex. The writers could convey these settings with authority because of their own experiences. And yet the setting of George Eliot's *Middlemarch*, in the English Midlands in the 19th century, is just as compelling, just as dramatic and full of interest. This was where George Eliot was raised as a child. This was her home. The setting is as vital and vibrant as the writing makes it.**

names in unspecified lands, we are still given details of the landscape and the age of the narrator. Location implies arrival, survival, possibly departure. Where did these people come from? How do they live? Often the answers to these questions are implied, rather than spelt out.

The setting in fiction is often used as a deliberate form of limitation. By removing freedom of travel or escape, fictional characters can be placed in unrelenting inter-relationships, and this facilitates drama. Think of *Robinson Crusoe* or *Lord of the Flies*. What do they have in common? Isolation on an island, which generates the drama that is the subject of each book. But the same effect can be obtained without a shipwreck.

Any drama of confinement limits the movement of people and thereby promotes a certain type of intensity - even if it is only intense boredom. A prison setting like Brendan Behan's *Borstal Boy* would be a classic example. In Kafka's *Metamorphosis*, Gregor is transformed into a giant bug and confined in his room.

Much writing about warfare uses the siege as its setting, and its fictional effect is parallel to the shipwreck. But dramas of confinement can be set anywhere: in a classroom, a bedroom, a hospital, an aeroplane. One form of fiction that has now arrived, and looks unlikely to depart, is that of enduring a terrorist hijack: history makes its contribution to fiction, whether we want it to or not.

Most writers are given their settings. Experience provides it, or curiosity stumbles upon it. Very few fiction writers set out self-consciously to discover new settings so that they can employ them in fiction. Both Evelyn Waugh and Graham Greene did precisely this: they found travel in foreign lands a stimulus that was necessary to motivate them to write.

The truth is that very few fiction writers these days would be able to afford to go off to Africa or Havana for six months, to get the feel of the place so as to write about it. Writers often write about the landscape and cities they know and were brought up in and worked in; think about Thomas Hardy's Wessex or William Faulkner's Yoknapatawpha County. These provide a world in themselves. Anything that can happen to anyone anywhere can happen to people in these demarcated worlds. It is a mistake to assume that one has to travel far to discover the exotic: the exotic is here, before us. Defamiliarization will make it come alive.

The setting is finally up to you as a writer. Remember that you must feel confident about moving your fictional characters around in it.

want to know more?

- Re-read any of the books mentioned in this chapter and look at how the writers conjure up their settings. In most cases you won't find long passages of description – just enough.
- We are in revolutionary Paris in the 1790s, are we? Prove it then. How do you as a writer do this? By astute research; by finding out exactly what you need to know to make such a fiction believable. See pages 170–74 for some advice on research.
- Whenever you travel anywhere, keep a notebook close to hand in which you record your impressions of the new place. Note tiny details like different kinds of bird call or what is being advertised on billboards.

4 Good writing

All good writing tends to place something before us in a manner that we have not expected. We see something a little differently. Otherwise, what would be the point of reading it? In fact, one characteristic of bad writing is that it doesn't do anything differently. It mechanically reproduces the existent, and the conventions for portraying it, and we are quickly bored. In this chapter, we will look at several different ways of keeping the writing fresh.

Good writing

Ezra Pound's advice about writing was simple: 'Make it new'. This does not mean pursuing novelty for its own sake, but it does mean avoiding cliché, and remembering Blake's advice: 'Always look through the eyes, not with them.'

must know

Dictionaries

Stare at words long enough and they will begin to speak to you. They will offer their services to the attentive writer. A good dictionary helps to translate what they are saying. Centuries of expertise are embodied in a dictionary. No writer can afford to ignore such a resource.

Defamiliarization

We do not have to travel to distant locations, either in time or space, to find the exotic. It is all around us. It is simply a question of the way we see things. Defamiliarization is the technique by which the daily, the ordinary, the mundane, become suddenly astonishing and strange. How does this come about? By seeing things differently through words, viewing reality from a slightly altered angle, so that what was previously settled and stable, now looks skew-whiff and unexpected.

Translated from the Russian word *ostranenie*, which means 'making strange', defamiliarization was one of the invaluable concepts developed by the Russian Formalists early in the 20th century. But it has always been there, in all good writing.

When the poet William Blake spoke of seeing through the eyes instead of with them, he was really talking about defamiliarization. What he meant by seeing *with* the eyes was being trapped inside conventions of perception, so that perception becomes an entirely expected activity, with its own predictable routines, instead of that cleansing of the doors of perception which is possible when we see through the eyes, when we let creation rush in and surprise us.

In Shakespeare's late play *The Tempest*, everything that happens is about defamiliarization. A shipwreck seems to drown all on board, but in truth none has been drowned; instead they 'suffer a sea-change into something rich and strange'. That is a very good definition of defamiliarization. Ariel says this to Ferdinand about his father:

Of his bones are coral made
Those are pearls that were his eyes.

What we don't expect to happen does in fact happen. We see transformations, metamorphoses. This is defamiliarization. And it can happen in fiction as effectively as it does in poetry and drama. The modern fiction known as Magic Realism is in effect a technique for the achievement of defamiliarization.

In Salman Rushdie's story 'The Prophet's Hair', cold water is described as having been given 'the cloudy consistency of wild honey'. That is defamiliarization. Something we all see many times a day looks different in an instant. A vivid perception has been transmitted, often by metaphoric transference. Vivid figures of speech are in fact forms of defamiliarization. So let us look for a moment at two of the most familiar of those figures of speech: metaphor and simile.

must know

Defamiliarizing tools

Metaphors and similes establish unexpected connections. They are a form of radical pattern-recognition. They are an essential tool of defamiliarization. But they must be striking; otherwise the writing will be slackened, not enhanced.

Metaphor and simile

Much good writing in both verse and prose achieves its effect through metaphor and simile. A metaphor says something is something else, and a simile says something is like something else. But they both see a parallel between one state of affairs and another, a parallel that is simultaneously just and unexpected. Once a metaphor ceases to be unexpected, it becomes a cliché. Good writers do not use clichés except to explode them, or to characterize the person using them as having a clichéd mind or tongue.

Let us take an example. At the beginning of John Gardner's novel *Grendel*, in which the monster who kills men in the Anglo-Saxon epic *Beowulf* is allowed to put his side of the story, Grendel is describing an old ram:

He cocks his head like an elderly, slow-witted king...

This is a simile; one thing is perceived to be like another. But why is it so effective? The ram is evidently perceived as not being the brightest of creatures, but it is territorial, and will not budge, despite being threatened by the monster with his fists and a rock. 'Elderly, slow-witted king' is a perfect way to describe this combination of stupidity and stubbornness. Both metaphors and similes are contractions of complex perceptions into single images.

If we think about it, we will see that metaphors and similes are both based upon radical pattern-recognition. Routine pattern-recognition is essential to our survival. If you do not know how to stop on the red light and go on the green, you won't be generating metaphors for long. But radical pattern-recognition is what permits true originality in the arts and the sciences.

One day, someone notices that the Bubonic Plague seems to arrive at the same time as those boats infested with rats. A connection is made. On another day someone else notices that the bite of the mosquito and the onset of malaria have a tendency to coincide. A pattern has been perceived. Once it is perceived, it soon stops being a radical pattern-recognition, and becomes instead a routine one. And the same thing happens with imagery in language.

When Burns first wrote that his love was like a red red rose, it was a radical connection. Now we have heard it so many times, it begins to seem trite. And it was the same when Shakespeare asked himself if he should compare his beloved to a summer's day. Good writing has to be constantly coming up with new images, fresh ways of thinking and writing; it cannot simply count on the collateral of those who have gone before. We must, as Pound exhorted us, 'make it new'. And that is precisely what Gardner has done here, in his image of the stubborn old ram as like 'an elderly, slow-witted king'.

Thomas Hardy wrote this:

...the real, if unavowed, purpose of fiction is to give pleasure by gratifying the love of the uncommon in human experience.

But what is common in human experience can also be made uncommon by defamiliarization.

Word awareness

We are now beginning to explore the essential fabric of the business of writing: language. This is any writer's ultimate resource. You should never be far from a good dictionary, the best you can afford. Ford Madox Ford used to give this advice to young writers: 'Read the dictionary. Find out what words mean.' No one can write well without developing a vast curiosity about language. Try to imagine a painter who has no interest in colour or form; that is a dismal notion, and so is a writer without an avid interest in language.

The English language is a resource of limitless riches. The fossilized poetry that already exists in it is waiting to be found. A dictionary is the limestone in which all these linguistic deposits can be examined. So let us look for a moment at 'word awareness', and how it permits not merely the expression of metaphors and similes, but their discovery too.

Word awareness

The aim of this simple example is to demonstrate what language starts to offer when it is quizzed and probed. The more inquisitively we examine words, the more they will provide their own help in the enrichment of the writing process. Choose your own straightforward sentences and see how you can improve them.

1. *Dorothy started to live alone again in January.*

Here the word 'January' is employed merely as reference. It is flatly denotative.

2. *There was something of January in Dorothy's bleak features.*

Here we are looking at a dormant metaphor. We have gone past denotation to connotation, but the connotative process has not really been either exploited or pursued.

3. *January was visible in Dorothy's features. Janus, the Roman god who had made a home of that word, had once more taken up his post as sentry of limits, borders, demarcations. One of his faces pointed back over the old year of disappointments and departures, already blank as snow, while the other looked forward to a new one, to a surging season with a fresh green language. There was still some uncertainty in her mind which of the god's faces she would choose to follow. Right now, he was resolutely staring in both directions at the same time. On certain days she felt nearly cross-eyed with confusion.*

Now the metaphor is actually coming alive; this is because it is being pursued with some energy. It finds such energy through a vivid word-awareness, a perception of the extraordinary amount of life locked in words. The language itself here becomes a provider of the writer's resources.

Language: the writer's choices

All writing is ultimately made out of three elements:

A. Vocabulary
B. Syntax
C. Punctuation

The words you choose, the order you put them in, and the marks that indicate how they should be read: this is writing, all writing, when we look at it formally. Whatever else you do, whatever else you think, these three elements will finally dictate what is written on the page, and therefore what is read there too. If something is wrong with your writing, then it will be because of your inadequacy in deploying these means. Let us therefore look at them one by one.

Anglo-Saxon and Romance words

Because of the history of Britain, the English language is made up primarily of Anglo-Saxon elements on the one side and Latinate or Romance elements on the other. Our language was originally overwhelmingly Teutonic, then the Norman invasion in 1066 brought with it the Romance element in the form of French. These two elements melded together until by Chaucer's time we have effectively the same form of English that we speak and write today.

This combination of different linguistic elements presents the writer of English with a unique resource. Getting the balance right between these different elements is a crucial aspect of good writing. Why? Because the words evoke different feelings, different connotations, different moods and different tones. Anglo-Saxon words have a homeliness, an earthiness, a daily potency about them, where the Romance words have a tendency to sound both grander and more abstract.

Here are a few simple examples of words that technically mean the same thing and yet feel very different depending on whether we go to the Romance or the Anglo-Saxon root:

- Preface/foreword
- Contradiction/gainsay
- Ancestor/forebear
- Improvement/betterment

All these words feel different, and assessing the weight, the specific gravity of words, is a substantial part of the writer's business, as is thinking about usage. Consider this curiosity. Only in English do we refer to the animal, using one linguistic lineage, and refer to the meat derived from it using the other:

- Cow/beef
- Deer/venison
- Pig/pork
- Sheep/mutton (though lamb is an exception to the rule)

Why? No one is quite sure. But the Saxon words denote the animal; the French ones the dish. We could only reverse the process in writing for comic effect: 'Would you like some more pig with your chips?' Similarly, if we compliment someone on their cuisine, we are talking about their cooking; if we say we like their kitchen, we are talking about interior decoration.

Language as fossil poetry

History and the history of meanings bury themselves in words. Etymology, or the study of the roots of words, digs them out again. The more the writer is aware of the history contained inside words, the greater is that writer's linguistic resources.

Let us look at a simple example. Take the word dandelion. It appears to describe a common enough phenomenon. And yet the word is full of linguistic delight. Because of the bright yellowness of the plant, and the tooth-like shape of its leaves, it was thought of as *dent de lion*, tooth of the lion. In the early 16th century, that was precisely how it would have been used in English, but a century later it had been anglicized into dandelion. The lion's tooth is still in there if you look.

Such looking is facilitated by the dictionary, the invaluable resource.

Syntax

First we must choose the words, then the order in which to put them. Each is equally important. Syntax is the musculature of prose; it is the manner in which vocabulary articulates itself. A good piece of writing will show syntactical variety and range; sentences will be of different lengths; subject, verb and the additional configurations will sometimes be reversed. Passive voicings will alternate with active ones. Adjectival and adverbial additions will never simply form predictable and repetitious listings.

Let us take a rudimentary example.

John liked to talk to Sally in the mornings. He would bring a cup of coffee up from the kitchen and give it to her while she lay in bed.

now you do it

Replace the obvious

Check your work for clichés and obvious phrases and replace them with more unusual word choices. Think of memorable ways in which you could replace the following:

- **piercing blue eyes**
- **cold as ice**
- **pearls of wisdom**
- **raining cats and dogs**
- **bright as a button**
- **a glowing sunset.**

He would sit on the side of the bed and murmur contentedly, while she chatted away and sipped.

Each of these sentences starts with the subject John, either with his name or with the pronoun 'he', which can be a grammatical substitute. The subject in each instance is followed by the main verb, and then the predicate, or rest of the sentence. This makes for syntactic predictability and, if it goes on long enough, for tedium. So why not introduce some syntactic variety?

Cup in hand, John would climb the stairs to their bedroom. Sally would sip and chatter while he sat on the bed beside her, murmuring contentedly. The morning talk. He always liked it.

The repetitions have been avoided, and variations of sentence structure have been introduced. Immediately the prose becomes more interesting to read.

Punctuation

The function of punctuation is to allow the eye to read unimpeded. Punctuation marks are directions to the reader to facilitate the understanding of the words on the page without confusion. They should maximize the writing's potency. Bad or inadequate punctuation leads to confused reading; one must go back to the beginning of the sentence to discover who or what the subject is meant to be, or one is left trying to fathom which adjective applies to which noun, which adverb to which verb. Syntax and punctuation work together to avoid such wastes of energy.

We have already looked at the opening of *Moby Dick*. Let us consider it once more, since it certainly deserves re-visiting, and this time remove the punctuation:

call me ishmael some years ago never mind how long precisely having little or no money in my purse and nothing particular to interest me on shore i thought i would sail about a little and see the watery part of the world it is a way i have of driving off the spleen and regulating the circulation whenever i find myself growing grim about the mouth whenever i find myself involuntarily pausing before coffin warehouses and bringing up the rear of every funeral I meet and especially whenever my hypos get such an upper hand of me that it requires a strong moral principle to prevent me from deliberately stepping into the street and methodically knocking peoples hats off then i account it high time to get to sea as soon as I can

What has happened? We no longer know when to stop and start. Punctuation functions like an alteration in the intonation of our voice while speaking, or those brief pauses that signify a separate clause or a parenthesis in normal conversation. Punctuation does the same thing, but in silence, on the page. So let us restore Melville's original punctuation:

Call me Ishmael. Some years ago – never mind how long precisely – having little or no money in my purse, and nothing particular to interest me on shore, I thought I would sail about a little and see the watery part of the world. It is a way I have of driving off the spleen, and regulating the circulation. Whenever I find myself growing grim about the mouth; whenever I find

now you do it

Full stop

Write a sentence that is at least 200 words long. Make the lack of punctuation contribute to the effectiveness of the piece. Maybe you are conveying the rushed character of someone's thoughts in a crisis?

myself involuntarily pausing before coffin warehouses, and bringing up the rear of every funeral I meet; and especially whenever my hypos get such an upper hand of me, that it requires a strong moral principle to prevent me from deliberately stepping into the street, and methodically knocking people's hats off – then, I account it high time to get to sea as soon as I can.

Now the sentences form natural units of sense and articulation. The punctuation indicates which sections to read at one take, and where additional information is being inserted, often forming a subordinate unit within the larger grammatical structure. See how much longer it took to read the unpunctuated version; punctuation aids the economy of writing, and consequently the efficiency of reading.

Some modern writers have abandoned punctuation, or much of it anyway, to considerable effect. The most famous example is probably Molly Bloom's soliloquy at the end of *Ulysses*. Joyce drops all punctuation except for capital letters for names and the first-person pronoun 'I'. The torrent of undivided prose that then ensues is meant to convey the torrent of Molly's thought, her 'interior monologue'. Hemingway used the same technique in some of his early writing, and Beckett employed it a great deal in his later work. It is a difficult technique to master, and is probably best employed sparingly, though the absence of punctuation from a child's letter, an email or a text-message, can obviously be used by the fiction writer for comic effect.

Sentences

Vocabulary, syntax and punctuation all end up inside sentences. Thinking about the writing of sentences is important. Let's return once more to the opening of *Moby Dick*, since our familiarity with it might be beginning to pay some dividends. (James Joyce told Samuel Beckett that the only way for one writer to truly study the work of another was to copy out the other's writing by hand; and the constant return to 'exemplary texts', to see how they work, to understand how they came to be so good, is a very good habit for a writer.)

Call me Ishmael. Some years ago – never mind how long precisely – having little or no money in my purse, and nothing particular to interest me on shore, I thought I would sail about a little and see the watery part of the world. It is a way I have of driving off the spleen, and regulating the circulation. Whenever I find myself growing grim about the mouth; whenever I find myself involuntarily pausing before coffin warehouses, and bringing up the rear of every funeral I meet; and especially whenever my hypos get such an upper hand of me, that it requires a strong moral principle to prevent me from deliberately stepping into the street, and methodically knocking people's hats off – then, I account it high time to get to sea as soon as I can.

One of the first things you will notice is that these individual sentences do not find their shape in isolation. Sentences are designed to sit next to other sentences; they react to them in tone and rhythm. An important aspect of writing sentences is adjacency: a sentence exists in the context of other sentences, and must respond to them and elicit a response in return.

The first sentence here consists of only three words, and it is a command, an imperative, but a friendly one: 'Call me Ishmael.' Not Mr Ishmael but Ishmael. We are going to be on intimate terms with the speaking voice governing this narrative. The staccato opening is vigorous and terse. And then immediately we start to be given information, more complex information than the simple matter of naming, complex matter necessarily contained in a much more complex sentence.

Some years ago – never mind how long precisely – having little or no money in my purse, and nothing particular to interest me on

now you do it

Describe your hand

Fiction is made out of sentences. Every single sentence you write either contributes to the potency of your fiction, or detracts from it. In fiction there is no such thing as 'an unimportant sentence'. Write a short description of your hand in a way that lets the reader know something about your character. Make sure none of the sentences is out of place or inessential.

shore, I thought I would sail about a little and see the watery part of the world.

We move from the present tense – 'Call me Ishmael' – to the past. *Some years ago*. We are recounting history, but this is no pernickety historian who is going to insist on chronicling every date and query. We are informed in a parenthetical aside – 'never mind how long precisely' – that we are not to insist on too much in the way of past precisions. The tale to be told is perhaps too urgent for that.

We have already gleaned that this is not a rich man because we are told that he had little or no money in his purse, and we have noticed before that he does not have any binding family ties since he tells us that he has nothing much to interest him on shore. So he goes to sea. By this means, it seems, he avoids melancholy and irritation. This is conveyed very powerfully by the figure of speech, the metaphor he employs: '...whenever it is a damp, drizzly November in my soul'. We are being given a great deal of information here in a very short space. So let's stop right there and look at what is going on in the individual sentences.

Good and bad sentences

A sentence exists to convey information. The information might be historical, emotional or geographical, but a sentence is a structured group of words that conveys some kind of information to us.

First rule then: if your sentence is conveying no information at all, then it is a bad sentence, however beautifully you think you might have fashioned it.

In fiction, a sentence must always convey something to us that adds to the sum total of the text. It can do this in many ways. It can do it by recounting factual information, as does the following statement: 'In 1939, Germany invaded Poland.' But it can also do it by the effective use of metaphor in conveying mood, as here in the phrase 'whenever it is a damp drizzly November in my soul...' All of the resources of language and figuration are possible in constructing sentences.

Already then we have three concepts we can use in thinking about sentences: information, adjacency and figures of speech such as metaphor and simile. Or, to put it another way, we can think of what is being conveyed, the matter of the sentence: information. We can think of the surrounding verbal landscape in which it finds itself: adjacency. Finally, we can think of the linguistic and rhetorical means we might employ to convey meaning and mood, such as metaphor; simile; understatement; hyperbole, and so forth: figures of speech.

The best sentences are those most economically constructed. The most effective sentences are syntactically constructed to gain maximum effect, employing vocabulary, including substitute words like pronouns, to keep repetition to a minimum, and punctuating precisely in order to achieve the greatest intelligibility.

So let's once more return to the basic materials out of which all sentences are constructed: vocabulary, syntax and punctuation. If something is wrong with a sentence, then it will be one or more of those three categories that constitutes the problem. The words you choose, the order you put them in,

must know

Tools of the trade

Speaking purely formally, fiction writing is made up of vocabulary, syntax and punctuation: the words chosen, the order they are put in, and the signs that tell us how to read. Incompetence here represents the ultimate incompetence; it is like a musician who can't play the right notes.

now you do it

Favourite words

Write a list of your ten favourite words. Do it quickly, without stopping to analyze. Then write ten lively sentences with one of your words in each.

and the way you punctuate them: those are the fundamental decisions any writer constantly makes in writing fiction. This is the nitty-gritty of composition.

The way in which sentences are constructed, and then placed in relation to each other, will be governed by those various demands we might summarize as follows:

Information – the matter to be conveyed, and its part in the narrative.
Adjacency – the context in which this sentence of the text finds itself.
Figures of speech – metaphor, simile, understatement, irony etc.
Economy of means – contraction, ellipsis, the substitution of pronouns for proper names.

In addition to all these, there is a simple process of reversal, which entirely alters the functioning of a sentence: active or passive constructions. The active construction – *Bill kicked the table violently* – emphasizes and foregrounds the active agent.

Learn from poets

Read plenty of great poetry and try writing your own. Examine the way poets pay minute attention to each individual word, the juxtaposition of words and the rhythm of phrases within sentences. All of these lessons will be valuable when applied to prose.

It makes use of narrative dynamism. The passive construction – *The table was then kicked by the defendant* – attempts to be dispassionate, scientific, scrupulously forensic. It deletes the dynamic element of the agent in order to be as objective as possible.

If I start a piece of writing with the phrase,

Jonathan was being repeatedly kicked by two boys

then I have made Jonathan passive by the grammatical construction. He might become active later – he might even become a vengeful vigilante – but at this moment he is passive.

All of our resources as fiction writers are finally deployed in the writing of sentences, however long, however short. We deploy words into these units. This is what we all do all day, whatever else we might be doing. For this reason our alertness to the problems of sentence construction, the avoidance of slackness and verbal or syntactic repetition, is crucial to our task.

If the sentences don't work, then nothing works; it's as simple as that. Whenever we read good fiction we are reading good sentences. It would be meaningless to say, 'This is a very good piece of fiction but the sentences in it are awful'.

Read the great writers. See how they do it. Study how they make their sentences live on the page. Do the same yourself.

want to know more?

- **To brush up your grammar and punctuation, read *Collins Good Grammar Guide*, *Collins Good Punctuation Guide*, *Fowler's Modern English Usage*, *The Oxford Style Manual*, and *Elements of Style* by William I. Strunk and E.B. White.**
- **Buy *Roget's Thesaurus* and use it to make more unusual word choices that will retain the reader's interest.**
- **See page 181 for advice on which dictionaries to use.**
- **For examples of perfect sentence construction, read the essays of George Orwell or anything by V.S. Pritchett.**
- **Compare Hemingway's sentences with those of Henry James. Think about why each works for the subject matter they deal with.**

5 The short story

What is the difference between a short story and a tale? A tale is essentially an oral form that happens to get written down. A short story is an essentially written form, which is sometimes 'read out loud'. That is the original difference, and it is a very important one. In this chapter we will look at some of the requirements of a good short story, many of which apply to longer pieces of fiction as well.

The short story

Some writers say that short stories are trickier to get right than novels, whether your work has a contemporary modern setting, a historical theme or it takes place in the future on the planet Zorg.

now you do it

Montage

Stories of modernity are often fragmented; this is because modernity itself is fragmented. Modern life does not present itself to us in continuous wholes. It is often a montage of unconnected fragments. Write a modern urban story using a fragmented montage style.

Modern experience

Most of us can 'tell' the story of Little Red Riding Hood, but we cannot 'tell' a story by Katherine Mansfield or Henry James. These have become written forms, with self-consciously writerly aspects to them. I might be able to give you a summary of the plot, but that is no way an acceptable account of the 'story'.

And by the time we encounter short stories by David Foster Wallace in *Brief Interviews with Hideous Men*, the footnotes that appear with great frequency are in fact only possible with a written form – there are no footnotes in tales, since footnotes work visually, not orally. You have to be able to see them on the page. Gutenberg's revolution transferred our human experience to print.

We need to be honest with ourselves here and acknowledge that this involves loss as well as gain. The modern writer needs to face up to modern reality. A great deal of contemporary writing is about our inability to share experience, about the immense difficulty we often have in communicating anything of ultimate significance. The German critic Walter Benjamin had a wonderful phrase for this: he called it the 'decay of experience'. He remarks how soldiers returning from the Great War had all too often been reduced to silence, and when their books of memoirs started to appear in the 1920s, it was not a sharing of experience, but a description of experiences that could not be shared; an account of an experience that seemingly negated 'experience' itself.

Such warriors' accounts of what went on in modern warfare were not translatable into 'tales' at all. Hemingway's story 'Soldier's Home' examines this theme. In Homer or *Othello*, the returning warriors immediately begin to tell their tale. Intriguingly, many of the combatants in the Great War suffered the form of neurasthenia known as mutism. They lost the ability to speak. This condition and its treatment is one of the themes of Pat Barker's *Regeneration*.

Benjamin's argument goes further, and is of great significance for the fiction writer today. He says that the quality of modern experience itself is disintegrative; that the fragmentation of modern experience results in montage, cinematic cuts, and fragmentary representation. Too much of the experience of modern life (particularly in the big city) is fragmentary for us to be able to ignore the fact. We walk down the street, see thousands of faces we will never see again, see a train filled with people we will never know. Overhead an aeroplane carries its modern cargo of people we don't know and never will.

All this is what we have started calling contingency – the unexpected, the unresolvable – and it can be related to plot by formal devices. These formal devices interrupt what would be the seamless narrative of a 'tale'; in the modern short story we tend to show how very few things are reliably 'continuous'.

must know

The modern form

The modern short story is often not 'the story of a life' so much as an acknowledgment that such a 'story' can never be told. The modern form is constantly querying its own credentials to give an adequate account of things.

In the pages that follow we will identify some of the basic forms of the short story. Most of these categories also apply to the chapter on the novel that follows.

Monologue

The short story is a perfect setting for the monologue. This is not to say that it can't be used to great effect in the novel too. We have already mentioned John Gardner's *Grendel*, which is a monologue, and yet it is a monologue constantly interrupted by other conversations and outside reflections; which is to say that it is a 'novelized monologue'.

Let us look at two classic short stories written in the monologue form: 'The Tell-Tale Heart' by Edgar Allan Poe, and 'Deutches Requiem' by Jorge-Luis Borges. By the time we have read one page of each of them, we quickly realize what both have in common, apart from their first-person status. In each we hear a voice that might be against the world, or *contra mundum*, or that might perhaps be revealing the full extent of the unreliability of the narrator, including the possibility of madness.

When we discussed voicing we listed the attributes of the first-person mode as intimacy, bias, confidentiality and the impossibility of knowing everything. This last can become a crucial device. We only know what we are being told by the

Dramatic monologue

In the 19th century, Robert Browning wrote a particularly vivid type of poem that has come to be called a 'dramatic monologue'. It is often remarked how 'novelistic' some of these poems are, in their combination of specific social detail and the conveyance of character.

narrator, but there is always the possibility that we start to mistrust this information. If the narrator becomes an 'unreliable narrator' then that means we regard the information he is providing as tainted. This is precisely what happens in Poe's 'The Tell-Tale Heart'. The murderer hears the sound of the heart of the murdered man continuing its ghastly beat; but what we are actually hearing is the sound of insanity.

Although Poe's story is a melodramatic and lurid example of the genre, it is not different in principle from what Alan Bennett is doing in his *Talking Heads* series. Here once again we hear a monologue, and the monologue, while telling us one thing, starts to reveal another beyond the conscious wish of the narrator. Nearly all of his narrators are unreliable narrators.

Borges is one of the masters of the modern short story. He has enriched the form beyond measure. In 'Deutches Requiem' he presents us with Otto Dietrich zur Linde, a man with a noble lineage in German military history. He is meditating upon the significance of his life, which will shortly be coming to a close, since he is to be shot the following morning, having been condemned at the Nuremburg Trials as a Nazi, a torturer and a murderer. Unlike Albert Speer, Hitler's architect, Linde does not attempt to exonerate himself, or to say that he never understood how bad things were out there in the Reich. On the contrary, he embraces his fate. He refused to speak at his trial, but now feels free to write the words that we are reading – he tells us that he can speak without fear, for he says that he has no desire to be pardoned. He also points out that he feels no guilt. He simply wishes his part in history to be understood.

The short story in monologue form is the perfect vehicle for such a confession. Its intimacy can endow it with the quality of a softly-spoken deposition; as such, it allows for a particular, even a peculiar, testimony. We feel that we are not being declaimed at from a rhetorical pulpit. In fact, we are overhearing a monologue, and this quality of overhearing

now you do it

The unreliable narrator

The monologue is by its nature uninterrupted by anything except the reader's questions. If those questions grow loud enough, then we are dealing with the unreliable narrator. Try writing a first-person story told by an unreliable narrator.

gives it its sense of authenticity. We might think of it as the non-stage version of a soliloquy, in which we hear an actor speaking to himself while we are listening in.

Borges' protagonist Linde is able to see even the defeat of Germany and his own death as part of a larger scheme which will ultimately succeed. The hypocrisy of the ages, the Judaeo-Christian poison, has at last been swept away; in their place violence has asserted its rule. He ends by looking in the mirror and saying that his flesh may feel fear but he does not.

To see the effectiveness of this form for the writer we only have to imagine how different this story would be if it were told in the third-person. It would no longer be possible to enter so vividly into Linde's moral and psychological world.

An alternative strategy is that of Kafka in 'Metamorphosis', where some distance is required from the metamorphosed protagonist, so we have 'One morning Gregor Samsa woke to discover that he had turned into a giant beetle.' If this were presented in the first-person, we would probably assume the protagonist was mad. Which is precisely what we do assume (and rightly) in the case of the protagonist in 'The Tell-Tale Heart'. Which heart it is that tells the tale is open to question, but not for long. All the effects that this form facilitates would be rendered impossible if it were converted from monologue to duologue.

The Duologue

The duologue offers more potential drama than a monologue, because two voices are involved instead of one, and therefore two worlds are implied in those voicings. One version of reality can be contradicted. The word means gainsaying, saying against – *contra dictare*. Let us look at two versions of this technique: 'Proofs of Holy Writ' by Rudyard Kipling, and the Sherlock Holmes stories by Arthur Conan Doyle.

Kipling's story 'Proofs of Holy Writ' has Shakespeare sitting with Ben Jonson in a garden in 1610. There has always been a rumour, or a speculation, that Shakespeare had a hand in writing the Authorized Version of the Bible, sometimes called the King James Version, which was published in 1611. All sorts of clues have been found, often by those known as anti-Stratfordians – those who do not believe that William Shakespeare of Stratford-upon-Avon wrote the works attributed to William Shakespeare.

Here is one of the more cryptic clues. In the King James Version of the Bible, in Psalm 46, the 46th word from the beginning is 'shake' and the 46th word from the end is 'spear'. The Bible had taken six years to complete, and was completed in 1610, when Shakespeare was forty-six years old. This might have been his signature in the masonry, in the manner of medieval builders who carved their own face into a wall.

The 'proofs of holy writ' in the punning title are the unfinalized versions of the Bible. Ben Jonson and Shakespeare sit at a table in a garden. They drink wine; they joke; they mock one another. They are old troupers, old professionals in the theatre business. They set about improving one of the translations of Isaiah out of the Latin version.

now you do it

Dialectics

In fiction two people arguing are involved in what the Greeks called dialectics: a quarrel that reveals the nature of reality. Write a dialogue in which the protagonists are arguing. Remember that in arguments people rarely listen to what the other person wants. Try to make clear to the reader what each of your characters is most concerned about, even though they might not be aware of it themselves.

now you do it

Two world views

The duologue must contain variety, even contrariety. There is no point having two identical voices speaking to each other. Two worlds must meet, and sometimes collide. Write a duologue between two people who are stuck in a queue.

Shakespeare explains the nature of the game:

You know this business as well as I. The King has set all the scholars of England to make one Bible, which the Church shall be bound to, out of all the Bibles that men use.

Ben Jonson is a little put out that he has not been contacted, since he regards himself as being by far the better scholar. But as the duologue proceeds, we come to understand that Shakespeare is by far the better writer. He is the one whose rhythms and vivid phrases light up the enterprise.

We see here one of the uses to which the modern writer has put the short story: it can be a form of historical speculation; a way of investigating some small possibilities that have never emerged in the written record. And here it is accomplished in the duologue form.

If we think about it, we will see that the duologue is the overall form of a great many of the Sherlock Holmes stories. There is a constant conversation taking place between the relatively slow-witted, if good-hearted, Watson, and the mercurial intelligence and unpredictable temperament of Holmes. Watson's clumsy assays at the truth provide Holmes with the perfect foil he needs to prove his extraordinary ability at deduction. Holmes has a great deal of darkness inside him; Watson acts as a homely candle waiting for the next lightning flash.

Epiphany

It was James Joyce who introduced this word into the practice of modern fiction. He borrowed it from the Christian tradition, where the Feast of the Epiphany is the occasion when the infant Jesus is first shown to the world. The Magi, or three wise men, arrive from the East to see this child-phenomenon. Their worldly wisdom is confronted with a supernatural power before which they bow down.

It is therefore a 'showing-forth', the revelation of a reality in a dramatic situation. Joyce borrowed it and made its sacred implications profane. Any moment between people, or even within people, that shows forth a truth, becomes an epiphany.

In *A Portrait of the Artist as a Young Man*, Joyce has his protagonist discussing this concept, and its relevance for art. To portray a situation in which such a showing-forth occurs is a substantial part of the writer's work. The short story is of a perfect length to permit the revelation of an epiphany.

In his collection of short stories *Dubliners,* each story manages to show forth a particular, if complex, truth. People and situations reveal themselves through gesture and speech, through silence and expression; the truth of the situation is expressed by its fastidious portrayal. Joyce described his prose technique in *Dubliners* as one of 'scrupulous meanness': he would portray the paralysis of that European city of half a million souls – a city he loved and detested in equal measure. The 'showing-forth' can be allowed to speak for itself. The snow that falls at the end of 'The Dead' is perfectly emblematic of all failure and tragedy.

must know

Revelation

The epiphany works by showing forth a particular truth. This is an effect of the behaviour and words of the people in the story. The revelation needs to be conveyed with clarity.

The miniaturized biography

Many stories naturally take the form of a small biography: 'John Kettle was born in the town of

must know

Showing v. telling

The miniaturized biography must be economical with its information and its images – this is the key to its effectiveness. Find images, significant moments, to convey character. Don't say 'Jonathan was careful about money.' Say 'Once a month Jonathan tore open the envelope containing his bank statement with the avidity of a lover opening the longed-for letter.' That *shows* instead of *telling*.

Huddersfield fifty years ago...' This is as predictable an opening in its way as 'Once upon a time...' But there are some classic examples of the short story as a miniaturized life, and one of the greatest of all is 'Un Coeur Simple' or 'A Simple Heart' by Flaubert, originally published in 1875 as one of three stories in the book *Three Tales*. This little book was the most popular one that Flaubert ever published in his lifetime. This utterly astonished him – but then the writer's life can be an astonishing business.

'A Simple Heart' is the story of Félicité, the servant who spends her life looking after her employer – with whom it is not always easy to get along. The servant had been disappointed in love long ago, and is now both devout and devoted, dedicated to her religion and her work. Her one true companion is her parrot Loulou. The servant loves this bird and when it dies, she has it stuffed by the taxidermist so that together they may continue to occupy the same space they always have. Towards the end of Félicité's life the Holy Ghost, who is often portrayed as bird-like in Christian iconography, becomes entirely associated in her mind with the parrot; the two become indistinguishable.

The end of the story has Félicité dying and seeing in a vision of glory the bird – now entirely made one in her mind with the third person of the Trinity. What is remarkable about Flaubert's achievement here is that he never bends into irony. The writer famed for his dyspeptic and analytical portrayal of the idiocies of modern life (*Madame Bovary* was tried for obscenity in 1857) is here non-judgmental, even sympathetic. Félicité has her own nobility, on which he as a writer will not encroach. This miniature biography has also become an epiphany. It would be hard to summarize, but we might say that individual perception is to be allowed its potential grandeur, even when it is based upon delusion.

The short story as puzzle

The short story as puzzle is one of the most popular and enduring of forms. One of its quintessential manifestations is the detective story, though Borges plays with the form, and turns it into a species of metaphysical speculation, in stories like 'Death and the Compass'. This particular type of writing is usually dated back to 'The Murders in the Rue Morgue' by Edgar Allan Poe. Dupin in that story solves a seemingly insoluble crime. He does this by dispensing with unnecessary presuppositions and unhelpful hypotheses. In this we should remember he is embodying the modern scientific method. Sherlock Holmes, too, was greatly given over to modern techniques of detection and analysis.

It is characteristic of the modern detective in the modern detective story that he or she regards as hypothesis what others around them regard as fact. The fundamental unexamined hypothesis in the Poe story is that the perpetrator of the crimes in the Rue Morgue is human. Dupin starts to see that the apparent impossibility of getting in or out of the apartment, and the stuffing of a woman's inverted body up a chimney, suggest a different sort of perpetrator: an orang-utang. What he has done is to dispense with unnecessary presupposition; all he needs to do now is to find the sailor who had acquired the beast in some far-off place and brought it to the city, where it escaped.

must know

Untangling the threads

We delight in the demonstration of unrestrained intelligence. We know that life is complex and knotted; one pleasure fiction affords is to have one small part of the thread unknotted for us. The detective is an exemplification of the principle of intelligence in fiction. His motto could be E.M. Forster's little phrase: 'only connect'.

must know

Character development

Short stories often fail because they attempt too much character development in the limited space available. On the whole, in the short story form, characters become more fully what they are, rather than radically altering.

This technique is famously encapsulated by Sherlock Holmes when he says that when you have dispensed with all the impossibilities, then what you are left with must be the truth, however improbable it might appear. The method of Sherlock Holmes has its own scientific antecedent: Professor Bell at Edinburgh University, where Conan Doyle studied medicine.

Bell was a brilliant pathologist who had a radical technique. The evidence was always there, he believed, if the data presented were to be read properly, i.e. without unnecessary presupposition. An example given – one later incorporated into a Sherlock Holmes story – is that of Bell examining a pocket-watch to discover the characteristics of its owner. Bell looked at the watch carefully for a moment, examining it through a magnifying-glass. He then declared the owner to be a person of some means, who had fallen intermittently on hard times and had taken to drink. How did he deduce all this? The watch had been an expensive one, not something any poor man could have easily owned. But it showed signs of having been pawned on more than one occasion – little marks registered its pawnings and its subsequent redemptions. So the man had needed money badly enough to pawn such a valuable possession. Lastly, the escutcheon around the keyhole had been badly scratched over and over again, suggesting a fumbling motion with the key. The owner was well-acquainted with drink.

It is exactly this technique that allows Holmes on meeting a client he has never seen before to deduce that he is a violin-player: the fingernails on his left hand are cut shorter than those on his right. Whatever appears miraculous about the technique of Holmes turns out to be nothing more or less than scientific method. He makes himself an expert in all kinds of fields: paper types, weapons, inks, tropical diseases, modes of transport. Then he simply dispenses with unnecessary hypotheses.

G.K.Chesterton in the *Father Brown Stories* continued the tradition, though the expertise of Father Brown himself is really concerned with human motivation. The real-life basis for the fictional character was Father (later Monsignor) John O'Connor, a parish priest in Keighley when Chesterton met him early in the 20th century. The two men walked together over Ilkley Moor and Chesterton was astonished by the priest's knowledge of humanity, his light-hearted appreciation of the corruptions of which our species is capable. It seems that O'Connor would have agreed with W.H. Auden: 'The desires of the heart are as bent as corkscrews.'

So the unnecessary hypotheses this investigator dispenses with are those associated with a modern humanistic view of the world: that progress is at work everywhere, that a modern philanthropist is likely to be a good man, that people usually say what they mean, even to themselves. And the great advantage of a figure like Father Brown, unlike that of Sherlock Holmes, is that no one imagines he is likely to have much intelligence. He is a shabby, almost ridiculous figure, as he bumbles about; so he effectively travels incognito.

The real hero of all these stories of detection is the intellect itself. Intellectual deduction is the

now you do it

Detection

Many of the great fictional detectives have contradictory characteristics; for example, they might appear bumbling but they are actually acute. All fictional creations benefit from some ambiguities. Invent three or four anti-heroes who have both good and bad qualities, and write a short description of each.

Ariadne's thread that leads us to the truth of the monstrous event. The labyrinth of modern experience is navigated by certain principles of decoding. As with Professor Bell's watch, a dialogue is set up between the constellation of the evidence and the original causes of those marks that have been left.

Ghost stories

The ghost story in one form or another is an enduring form. Many ghost stories are stories of place. The ghost appears as the trace of an event, a happening often from long ago, which has embedded itself into a specific topography. For example, the stories of M. R. James tend to be set in old cathedral towns. It is the unlocking of certain buildings, the entering of certain rooms or crypts, that tends to awaken the unquiet spirit.

Ghosts are like peculiarly potent memories, embodied memories, of a crime or an unhappiness that has never been exorcised. Those who encounter the ghost are encountering history, a history that could not be entirely repressed. The ghost then is often like Freud's neurotic symptom: it is the return of the repressed. It is intriguing how often a ghost, or the legend of a ghost, marks the site of an injustice, often a murder, or a wrongful execution, or a sexual injustice perpetrated by one with power on one without it.

Freud describes the uncanny as the meeting-point of the familiar with the unfamiliar; there is a sense of recognition combined with a sense of the unexpectedly sinister. This is often effected by the agency of darkness. A building, a home, a school, a church, which is familiar and comforting in daylight, becomes unpredictable and menacing in the darkness. Ghosts are the agencies that are entirely at home in the dark; their messages from the past are uttered out of obscurity. Obscurity is where they live, and yet they are still prompted to bring the past to light.

Character in short stories

Usually, stories tend towards the revelation of character rather than the development of it. If we think about this for a moment, it becomes evident that what happens to character in fiction depends upon the form in which the character is placed.

In a novel, character can develop and even change, though there must still be recognizable characteristics between the beginning of the narrative and the end. Think of Pip in *Great Expectations*: he undergoes a moral education, which complicates reality, and throws into a poor light his own snobbery towards those who raised and endowed him. He's still entirely Pip though; we live with him long enough to understand the changes he undergoes.

But in a short story there is usually only time enough for character to be exemplified rather than modified. The circumstances contrive just so much of a revelation that we understand someone to be thus and thus, even if the introductory description had concealed the true nature of his or her actual character from us.

In Scott Fitzgerald's story 'Basil: The Freshest Boy' we are surprised by the ending; the character has more 'character' than we had anticipated, but we then realize that it always lay concealed as a potential within him. His superficial unpopularity concealed an underlying strength that is only fully revealed to us at the end. This characteristic might be pushed to its limit in Ernest Hemingway's 'The Short Happy Life of Francis Macomber', but a story of such length is inching towards the novella form, and in any case what we witness at the end is a sudden and radical turning away from one sort of behaviour towards another, rather than a gradual transformation.

now you do it

The dark side

Why write? To find words for the unnameable and explore the darkness. Carl Jung said that to achieve what you want you have to go into the place you fear the most. Write about whatever this means to you.

In his novella *The Turn of the Screw,* Henry James returned to the theme of the ghost story with a very modern, critical cast of mind. He gives us a story in which we can believe in the existence of Peter Quint and his ghostly companion Miss Jessel, or we can believe that the present-day governess is in the process of going mad, and that it is her fantasy (caused perhaps by sexual frustration) which is generating the phantoms. We are faced here once again with the potential problem of the unreliable narrator.

The return upon a larger theme

It is interesting how often the modern short story returns upon a larger theme, from a very specific or even local direction.

We saw how Kipling had done this with his Shakespeare story, 'Proofs of Holy Writ', and he is far from alone in approaching this subject. Borges explored the Shakespeare theme in a number of stories.

In one truly brilliant example, 'The Memory of Shakespeare', written towards the end of his life, a man is given the memory of the Elizabethan. He is a modern man, and what happens is that he starts to perceive modern reality as though he were the Elizabethan playwright. It becomes confusing, and finally terrifying. Experiences become more intense than they ever were, and also more frightening. He begins to sense that inner darkness which many have surmised must have possessed Shakespeare, since how could he otherwise have made such extraordinary visits to the dark parts of the psyche that we find in the great tragedies? Finally, like the man who first gifted it to him, he wants to get rid of it too. The gift has become a curse.

When Angela Carter explored Shakespeare in her story 'Overture and Incidental Music for *A Midsummer Night's Dream*', she was primarily interested in the theme of androgyny; how men can also be women, women also men. It is the sexual ambiguities that can be found in the play which fascinate her.

A theme as large as Shakespeare is inexhaustible. Writers are always finding something new there, and the short story has been a classic form for their explorations.

Where novels can be vast, even at times rambling, short stories need to retain their focus. They are sprints rather than marathons. The focus is often, though not always, one particular person; all the other fictional characters are relevant insofar as their lives have an impact on this one person.

This is very much the case in the miniaturized life. In the duologue form we focus on two people, though one of them is frequently a foil to reflect the other's brilliance. This is certainly the case in the Sherlock Holmes stories where Watson's slow-witted dependability is the backcloth before which his brilliant friend capers; but it is also the case in 'Proofs of Holy Writ'. The epiphanic story shows us a constellation of humanity, and the working out of that configuration displays and exemplifies a human truth.

The monologue often feels like a natural form for a story, because it permits one voice to give us a version of reality in a concentrated form.

want to know more?

- **To write good short stories, start by reading lots of them. Try Chekhov. Even Tolstoy liked Chekhov's short stories, though he told him that his plays were 'worse than Shakespeare's'.**
- **Jorge Luis Borges is another writer for whom the brevity and condensation of the short story seem indispensable.**
- **David Foster Wallace is a contemporary writer who finds the story the most congenial form to work in; it permits him the tricksiness and ventriloquism which display his skills to their best.**
- **If you want to offer one of your short stories for publication, look at the magazine listings in *The Writers' Handbook* or *The Writers' and Artists' Yearbook* (see page 181). Follow the specifications they give regarding length and theme, as well as the submission requirements.**

6 The novel

The most obvious difference between a novel and a short story is length. The novel is so much longer, and all other differences arise from that fact. This greater length allows for a variety of voices, portrayals of many different lives in detail; it permits the description of lots of locations and their local populations. The narrative can speed up, slow down, have long meditative sections where little happens except a great deal of thought. The novel is perhaps the most flexible literary form ever invented; it delights in its ability to take on reality in any shape or form and transmute it into fiction. There is only one absolute rule: it must be compelling.

The novel

Novels come in all shapes and forms, some based on fact and others entirely invented. But they all have some characteristics and aims in common.

must know

Wickedness

'Pictures of perfection make me sick,' Jane Austen reveals in a letter. They also tend to lack energy, and it is energetic portrayal that we remember in fiction. We sometimes forget the good people in Dickens, but we never forget the evil ones. Much fiction is preoccupied with the revelation of wickedness. The novel is in love with life in all its mischievous variety, but never with perfection.

Characteristics of the novel

The great Russian critic Bakhtin identified a number of characteristics of the novel. Unlike epic, it is engaged with modernity, with the open-ended story of what is happening now in the world. The *story* in modern fiction, in other words, is not already 'closed'. Bakhtin gives an interesting example of the contrast. The *Iliad* starts with the rage of Achilles and ends with the burial of Hector; but this could not be the plot of a novel. A novel would somehow have to 'novelize' the events into a meaningful unity of action, but the epic faces no such requirement.

While looking at plot we saw how story (the original data or mythic material) has to be turned into plot. And yet in epic there is really no distinction between story and plot; everyone knows the story, and therefore there is no tension between the known and the unknown. In consequence, there is no required sequencing of information. Everyone already knows that Achilles will kill Hector, that Priam will weep for the return of his son's body, and that he will eventually be granted that privilege, after much pleading. There will be no twist in the tale. The epic poet's task is verbal enrichment, not narrative complexity.

But the novelist somehow needs to capture the openness, the contingency, of life as it is lived in the present. They need to capture something of the 'talk of the time' and the sense of the life of the time, its lack of resolution; the language of contemporaneity needs to enter the fictional world of the modern writer, even if the narrative is pushed back in time into a historical novel, or forward in time into a science fiction narrative. For fiction to come alive it needs to confront contingency, and somehow incorporate it into the writing.

Contingency (which we defined as what might happen but doesn't have to) is so much a part of modern life that it is inevitably a large part of modern fiction too. If we say of a piece of writing that it is 'over-plotted' or 'mechanical', then we are effectively saying that its necessary contingency has been banished; that causality (the kingdom of rules, the manipulated plot) has been allowed untrammelled reign, as though we were living in the realm of myth or epic, instead of that of fiction.

So the novelist must be open to experience, and the novel must negotiate the fragmentariness, the unexpectedness, of reality. The reality of modern life is that there is so much that we don't *know*. Another contrast that Bakhtin registers between the epic world and the novelistic one is the question of humour.

Humour is an effect of closeness; it is the abolition of distance between ourselves and a certain figure that lets us laugh at that person; any hierarchy that might have existed between us has been annihilated. If a man in a morning-suit wearing a top hat slips on a banana skin, the distance he would like to maintain between ourselves and him, the status he wishes to occupy, has been evacuated.

must know

Thackeray

William Makepeace Thackeray thought human beings were a bad lot on the whole (he included himself in the denunciation), and his fiction expressed this view forcibly. He felt that no one came out of *Vanity Fair* very well, and he was glad that they didn't, since this constituted his 'realism'. He was always explicit about his commitment to unhappiness in fiction: 'I want to leave everybody dissatisfied and unhappy at the end of the story – we ought all to be with our own and all other stories.' So: no artificially imposed resolutions here. The novel writer has no obligation to pretend that everything always turns out for the best. 'If only things had turned out differently,' we say. But we know in our hearts that it has always been in the nature of things not to.

The epic always places a certain distance between ourselves and the characters portrayed. It is a characteristic effect of fiction to bring us closer and closer to the protagonist, until even the last barrier is removed and we find ourselves inside his head, sharing his thoughts, undergoing his emotions.

Bakhtin also points out that the novel is an omnivorous form, which is to say that it tends to swallow all the other genres and make them its own. We can see this if we look at Nabokov's *Pale Fire*. This book begins with a poem by the (fictional) poet John Shade, and the rest of the text is an unreliable reading of that poem by the demented Kinbote. In other words, the novel has created itself by cannibalizing a number of different genres: poetry, commentary, literary criticism, biographical memoir and autobiography. Such a hybridization of form is characteristic of the modern novel; it does not acknowledge any outer boundaries to its realm. It takes on all comers.

A novel such as Philip Roth's *The Human Stain* is simultaneously a love story, a political critique, a satire, a sexual manifesto, and a meditation on race and identity. It is also a lament for an educational system that has sacrificed independence of thought in the name of ideological permissibility.

Solitude and silence

People argue about when the novel form was first developed. What is not in dispute is when it first entirely flourished; this was in the 18th century. It has never ceased flourishing.

Every time someone announces the death of 'print culture', more books of fiction seem to appear by way of resurrection, despite the best attempts of certain book-sellers to separate the commodity-status of books from anything approximating to their intellectual content. There is an engaging little book by the Hungarian photographer André Kertesz called *On Reading*. Every image shows someone reading, usually a book. On trains, in cafés, in parks, on the street, by a window, people young, old or somewhere in-between, read, and the act of reading separates them into a silence and a solitude that puts them in a world entirely of their own. The novel form, perhaps uniquely, is designed to be enjoyed in solitude and silence, and that is how it is normally created, too. The American novelist James Baldwin claimed that his first novel was largely written in noisy bars, but this experience is the exception not the rule.

All the voices, all the monsters of hilarity and cruelty, the demonically-driven or the inexplicably serene, the killers, the killed, the impotent and the priapic, are created on the page in silence by a solitary labourer known as a writer. It is curious that there has been such a fashion for biographies of novelists in the last few decades, since most novelists' lives consist of sitting at a desk for most hours of the day, creating characters and voices. Melville went whaling, Hemingway hunted and fished and went to war, Dickens endured the blacking factory, but most fiction writers for most of their lives give themselves over to the generation of words. In solitude and silence.

No acknowledged borders

What is extraordinary about the novel is its illimitability. Whatever can be found in other forms, it will take and use for its own purposes. It does not acknowledge genre boundaries, which has led to much confusion for the classifiers. Kurt Vonnegut has

now you do it

Empathy

What is it that makes some characters sympathetic while we instantly dislike others? Often, we like them when we recognize their humanity. Think of some ways to introduce a character that would make the reader empathize with him or her straight away.

often complained how from the first he was classified as SF, which was a way of discounting the undoubted intellectual content of his work. Though it has to be said, it doesn't appear to have done his sales any harm.

We can be on an island, apparently alone, separated from all the civilities of social life. We can be in an English country house, attempting to ascertain, by the length of certain parentheses, what is going on in certain cultivated minds. We can be in a brothel in Rome during the Second World War, trying to work out whether the enemy we're fighting can really be any more insane than the comrades who fight by our sides. Or we can be in a rented room in North Kensington, naked, strapped to a rocking chair, attempting to establish the mind's power over the stimuli with which the world presents it.

This is the novel. It can even return upon itself, for purposes of elaboration, qualification, or contradiction. Michel Tournier's book *Friday* returns to the plot of *Robinson Crusoe*, to tell the story from the point of view of the other person on the island; Jean Rhys's *Wide Sargasso Sea* returns to the theme of *Jane Eyre*, to try to understand a little more about the relationships between finance, imperialism and sensuality in 19th-century Britain. In *Last Orders*, Graham Swift borrowed the form of William Faulkner's *As I Lay Dying* to explore a different sort of funeral ceremony. This has been going on from the very beginning: Henry Fielding's *Shamela* was a parodic response to Samuel Richardson's *Pamela*.

The mimicking of other forms for fictional purposes is a part of novelistic fiction's universalizing ambitions. Swift's *Gulliver's Travels* used the reports from the Transactions of the Royal Society to deadly effect, in giving accounts of Lemuel's journeyings and the goings-on at the Institute in Lagado. Remember, too, the relationship of the poem and the commentary in Nabokov's *Pale Fire*, or the 'official account' of Billy Budd's crime and execution in Melville's novella *Billy Budd, Foretopman*, followed by the sailors' song which gives a different account of things entirely.

Telling ourselves stories

Novels are about the different voicings of reality; the different accounts that we give of the nature of things; the way in which we all fictionalize reality, which is to say make it into stories, so that we can make sense of it. The narrative impulse is one of the most distinctive characteristics of human beings. We can see this very simply if we think of the way in which we describe non-organic bodies, such as the celestial variety.

We speak of 'the birth of a star' in nebulae, we speak of the life-span of a star, we speak of the 'face' of a star, or of its death in a white dwarf. We are writing the biography of a star, but a star has no 'biography'. It is not 'born', nor does it 'die'. We have turned it into a story, a life-story, so that we can tell that story. This is how we make sense of the world about us.

What is distinctive about the novel is the number of alternative, or even competing, stories that will be presented to us. A novel exemplifies our fictiveness; it shows how we can't help but render reality as a narrative, and how no two narratives ever entirely

must know

Dialogic

A story can give us one version of reality. It is in the nature of novels to give more than one, even in a first-person narrative: we hear other people's versions of reality in conversations, letters, speeches. This is that vibrant and negotiated quality of reality in the novel which Bakhtin called 'dialogic'.

agree. If they do, it will be through a suspicious collusion; as in forensics, so in fiction.

Bakhtin once more pointed out a salient characteristic of the novel: there will be competing versions of reality inside any good one. There may be an 'official version' of reality that the book is propounding, but it will (often despite itself) allow other versions to come forward, other voicings and perceptions, contrary visions that contradict even the views the author might hold.

Types of novel

There are all sorts of ways of describing novels. It should be said that these various ways of describing them don't necessarily help with their writing. But let us at least look at a few distinctions, ones that are essentially about the novelist's choices; about modes of writing.

If I contrasted two novels and said one was a social novel and the other a work of Magic Realism, I am almost certainly indicating a care for the scrupulous observation of social conditions and their effect upon 'characters' in one type of writing, whereas the other permits itself a freedom from constraint (however much social detail there may be), which lets the novelistic form intermingle with the fable.

Similarly if I talk about a psychological novel (the type of book that is sometimes called a *Bildungsroman*) then I am showing how the development of a protagonist is foregrounded by the writer to indicate that person's development, growth, education. We could think of classic instances like Charlotte Brontë's *Jane Eyre*, Joyce's *Portrait of the Artist as a Young Man*, or Proust's *Remembrance of Things Past*.

If I say that a novel is episodic, I'm saying that what holds it together is a series of episodes, all of which concern our central character; a good example would be Saul Bellow's *Adventures of Augie March*.

What came to be called 'documentary fiction', works such as *USA* by John Dos Passos or E. L. Doctorow's *Ragtime*, blends actual historical figures with invented ones.

There is even a species of novel that received the title of 'nonfiction novel'. The most famous example is Truman Capote's *In Cold Blood*. The 'novel' describes an actual series of killings. It does not invent, so much as elaborate.

And we might end with 'paranoid fiction', a type of writing exemplified by the American writers Thomas Pynchon and Don DeLillo. Such writing takes as its starting-point the deceitfulness of state authorities and sanctioned modes of communication. It assumes that fiction must begin its work by attacking and decoding the fictions that arrive in the name of ideology. The founding text of this school (its Magna Carta, if you like) is the Warren Report, which found that President John F. Kennedy had been killed by a solitary gunman, Lee Harvey Oswald. DeLillo's book *Libra* centres around this subject, and the seemingly endless possibilities for speculation it provides.

The difference between novels and short stories

We started by asking, what is the essential difference between a short story and a novel? Length, we said, and all that extra length facilitates. We might think of a specific example. Joyce had originally conceived *Ulysses* as a short story, a day in the life of Leopold Bloom in Dublin. What happened? The conception grew deeper and larger, and we ended up with the many hundreds of pages that now constitute the novel.

The biggest difference between a short story and a novel is the size and depth of the conception and execution. Greater complexity of characterization, plotting, counter-plotting, sub-plotting; social and historical setting; the long fictional movement through time – all give a novel a greater size and scope than the short story. Between the two lies the shadowy hinterland of the novella; this is a hybrid form, whose definition

now you do it

Writing about sex

Write not a 'sex scene' but a scene charged with erotic power. Use no obscenities; give no direct descriptions of a graphic nature. Let the movement of fingers, the tightening of lips, the touch of a fingernail across a skirt, convey the energy that can exist between two people.

often depends more on word-count than anything else. Conrad's *Heart of Darkness* is sometimes called a novella, sometimes a novel.

In a novel, as in its shorter relative, we are telling ourselves stories, but large, complex stories, stories that don't necessarily have any immediate resolution. Many characters come and go, live and die, do good or evil, or refuse to choose between them. And these are sexual creatures too. If any single change might be detected between the 19th- and the 20th-century novel it is a growing explicitness in matters of sexual depiction, and a growing laxity in regard to the employment of obscenity.

Obscenity is in fact a very difficult fictional mode to sustain with any conviction. It tends to become tiresome very quickly. The verbal variety moves rapidly towards lexical nullity, and the portrayal of sexual acts in lengthy graphic detail requires of the writer a skill which is all too often found lacking. Philip Roth seems to be the exception that tests every rule, but then Roth is one of the greatest writers of prose who has ever lived.

What is it that Roth does in books such as *Sabbath's Theatre*, *The Human Stain* and *American Pastoral* that makes them genuinely shocking? He employs language and intellect to question everything we hold dear, and perhaps even some things we hold cheap, but still hold.

Freud wrote a book usually translated as *Civilisation and Its Discontents*. The essential argument of this book is that the price for holding civilization together is the repression of our natural instinctive needs; such repression makes us ill.

Roth's novels ask with unremitting honesty, is it really worth it? His characters will not connive in the repression of their needs and instincts; their urges and desires spill out all over the place, causing social and marital mayhem as they go.

A character such as Micky Sabbath in *Sabbath's Theatre* is so insalubrious and morally repellent that we can only marvel at Roth's skill in gaining our sympathy for him. He does it as he does with other characters: by portraying a relentless truthfulness that all our civilities and equivocations simply cannot answer. We are here to copulate, his characters shout, yet all that awaits each one of us is not a bed, but a grave. We are psychologically designed to live for ever, yet each day we are confronted with the hooded hordes of the dead as they cross and re-cross our memories.

So what comfort is to be had? We tell ourselves stories. But they have to be highly intelligent, complex, troubled stories; otherwise we'd be lying to ourselves. We'd be pretending that we weren't modern.

The novel can never be defined, only explored. Every time a definition of it comes up, a different type of novel is written that was not included in the definition. Before Joyce wrote *Ulysses*, such a book had never been included in the definition of the novel. And that is even truer of his last book, *Finnegans Wake*. T. S. Eliot found himself wondering if the novel had ended, and if Joyce was returning to the epic form.

A novel such as Samuel Beckett's *The Unnameable* seems to be testing the form to destruction. William Burroughs experimented with his 'cut-up' technique, so that the arbitrariness, the contingency of modern life, could be incorporated directly into the writing

must know

Desolation

We have to hear intriguing and compelling voices, even if their subject is desolation. Philip Roth's novels are all about desolation, but they compel our attention. Similarly Beckett's fictions are about imprisonment, paralysis, inability, and yet the language, in all its stoical precision, always makes us laugh.

must know

Boy on a pier

You want to describe a boy on a pier in the 1950s, but you have no idea what it was like to be such a boy, because you have never been one, and you weren't even alive in the 1950s. So think like a novelist. What does a novelist do in such circumstances? Postcards are cheap. Most of them were sent from the seaside. Find one that portrays a pier and study it closely. The boy would probably have been wearing short trousers. Imagine the wind from the sea on his bare legs. In his pockets there would have been some coins. Go to a coin shop and ask to see the normal currency of the 1950s: hold the coins in your hand, feel the curious warmth of a large copper penny as it gathers the heat from your flesh. You don't have to buy anything, but you have just done enough research to provide you with pages of writing.

process. B. S. Johnson took this process one step further when he wrote a novel whose pages are interchangeable by the reader, so that contingency actually alters the way the plot pans out.

In comparison, in formal terms, Philip Roth seems relatively conservative. And yet the traditional form in his hands becomes so potent that it is hard to see how he can push his insights and his fury any further. But the furious insights continue to arrive, book by raging book.

The novel escapes definition. It is capable of anything. But it must be intelligent; it must use words with vividness and discrimination; it mustn't cheapen its characters into two-dimensions. It shouldn't rely on irony as an alibi. And it should always remain capable of surprising itself. Otherwise it will never surprise its readers.

The novel is a big enough form to create a world. This represents both the excitement it generates and the challenge it presents to the writer. Characters, even relatively minor ones, need to be convincing. The way they speak, dress, walk, drive, work, drink, cook – all are aspects of their characterization.

If we are slipping inside a character's mind by means of the free indirect style, then what goes on in that mental space needs to be convincing. The novelist tells us things about her characters, but these characters also have plenty to say about one another; the way in which people speak about one another is another essential area of 'research' for the serious novelist. A good writer is always engaged in research.

You are sitting at a table and someone remembers a grand lady she knew some years before:

I always used to think of Nancy as rather like Blackpool Rock. She was brittle, varnished, tasteless in her own saccharine way, a little vulgar, and wherever she snapped you knew there would always be writing through the middle, saying: BITCH.

A contribution to the novel has just been made.

Bakhtin described the novel as omnivorous; it swallowed all other forms and made them its own. It was fascinated with all forms of life, and constantly morphing to facilitate their portrayal.

This has one evident implication: the novelist too must be omnivorous, intellectually, emotionally and linguistically. We have to listen, observe, and take note of all of the available forms of life around us, since this is our material. The novelist's eye needs to be comprehensive, and the novelist's language as adaptable as the languages spoken out on the street.

want to know more?

• Documentary books, films, recordings, newspapers, even other fiction – as long as you take care to avoid plagiarism – all these are natural resources for the fiction writer to employ.

• See chapter 10 for advice on submitting novels for publication.

• On page 181 there is a list of useful websites for novelists.

• Do some bookshop research and try to work out how booksellers categorize books by genre. If you are writing in a genre, read lots of other examples to work out the 'rules'.

7 Irony

Irony is unavoidable. To live entirely without it would constitute either sainthood or idiocy. Our reality is fractured, and one of the ways in which the fractures express themselves is through irony. A person entirely devoid of irony would probably be tiresome, and the same applies to any substantial work of fiction.

Irony

The fiction writer should never use irony as an alibi, a way of getting himself off the hook of his own meaning. What do we mean by this? And how should irony be used?

must know

A Modest Proposal

Read 'A Modest Proposal' by Jonathan Swift. It's a foundational ironic text. The voice is calm, measured, equable. It is a rational voice, one we assume we can trust. Sentence by sentence we start to learn what the voice is recommending: infanticide in Ireland, to solve the problem of malnutrition. The ironic gap is vast and far from comfortable. Irony when charged with passion can be savage.

What is irony?

It is impossible to read much fiction without encountering irony. So what exactly is it? Put at its simplest, irony is the employment of words that do not mean what they claim to mean at the literal level. Exasperated at his companion's knowingness, a fictional character cries out,

Janet, when I get home tonight, I'm going to take all the encyclopaedias from my shelf and put you there instead. Then if there's anything I ever want to know, you'll be able to tell me, won't you, and I won't even have to waste time looking in the index.

The statement is ironic, because we know that this is not what the character will do. He knows it; even Janet knows it.

Irony, which comes from the Greek word 'to dissimulate', is a deliberately false statement, whose falsity registers not as a deception, but as an effect of distancing. 'You're a clever fellow, aren't you?' we say to the man who just fell into the pond while playing the fool. We mean, of course, the precise opposite of the obvious meaning of the words, and the drenched man knows it too.

For irony to work, there must be complicity; otherwise there is simply misunderstanding.

We have agreed to let literal meanings dissimulate the surface of expression, because we can see behind that surface a subtler intention at work.

Let's go back again to the opening of *Pride and Prejudice*:

It is a truth universally acknowledged, that a single man in possession of a good fortune, must be in want of a wife.

If you do not smile, however bleakly, at that statement then you might not be Jane Austen's ideal reader. If you cannot register the irony here then presumably you must either accept the justice of the remark, or beg to differ. In either instance you are imperceptive of the gap that is opening up between the apparent meaning of the words and the possibility of an intentional reversal that lurks immediately beyond.

So what do writers use irony for? They use it for humorous effect, most obviously. So we have the story of the rich little French girl who was asked in school one day to write a short story about a poor family. She duly began:

The Boissons were a very poor family. The father was poor. The mother was poor. The children were poor. The cook was poor. The gardener was poor. The nanny was poor. Both chauffeurs were poor. And as for the butlers...

What is the ironic effect here? It is the impossibility of the rich girl imagining an actual state of poverty, so although she intends no irony, her words achieve it anyway, by contradicting with each successive clause that original designation

must know

Irony and sincerity

Casual irony is the easy option for a writer. It's much harder to find a form of sincerity that doesn't sound naïve or cloying. A writer must use irony for effect, not for self-protection.

'a poor family'. A distance is opening up, an ironic distance, between her notion of poverty and her expectations in regard to any form of existence.

But irony can also be savage, particularly when it is being used for satirical purposes. By praising what we actually detest, or disparaging what we truly admire, satirical irony draws attention to injustice, cruelty or stupidity. A classic example is Jonathan Swift's 'A Modest Proposal'. Here the irony begins in the title itself, for what the writer of this document is recommending is a solution to the problems of poverty and starvation in the Ireland of Swift's time, which is in fact far from modest: the solution is the cooking and eating of the children of the Irish poor. This legendary piece of writing is ironic from beginning to end, and the irony permits a silent cry of pain at the wickedness humans can inflict on one another. One of the advantages of his recommended scheme, our proposer writes, is as follows:

Men would become as fond of their wives during the time of their pregnancy as they are now of their mares in foal, their cows in calf, or sows when they are ready to farrow; nor offer to beat or kick them (as is too frequent a practice) for fear of a miscarriage.

Here the distancing ceases to produce an easy laugh. The distancing effect that irony generates can also induce a kind of vertigo. We find ourselves staring down at the opening gap between surface meaning and its tonal contradiction, and wondering if we might be about to fall in.

Irony: the modern dilemma

For the modern writer the question is often not whether to adopt irony, but how to escape it. Why is this? Irony opens up a space between our representation of reality and any real certainty about it. It makes us wonder to what extent we can take the writer's version of reality on trust. In modernity, where we live, we often find it difficult to decide whether or not there can be any firm foundation for our representations, and consequently whether or not there can be any firm foundation for our beliefs about existence: this is part of the curse of being modern, but also part of its philosophical excitement. One of the consequences of this is the generation of irony.

At the end of *Billy Budd*, Melville tells us that prior to the account he has just given of the tragic young foretopman's life, the only official version of the events leading up to his execution is entirely erroneous, accusing Billy of being a foreign agent (which he wasn't); of using a dagger to kill Claggart (instead of his bare fist); and describing Claggart as a dutiful son of the realm (instead of the monster of duplicity and resentment he actually was). All this is presented to us without comment. It is simply the way things are:

The deed and the implement employed sufficiently suggest that though mustered into the service under an English name the assassin was no Englishman.

None of this is true, but it has become 'the official account'. But then there is another account of Billy in a sailor's song, an account that presents him as something close to a saint. And between the two radically variant accounts, there is the text of *Billy Budd* itself. No sense is given that there is likely to be any ultimate reconciliation between these different versions of events.

Here we have something approaching what philosophers call 'infinitized irony': the sense that there is no ground that will secure all the floating meanings and variant readings. The ironic distance between appearance and reality is never healed; there is no agency potent enough to effect such a healing. This is very much our modern dilemma as writers of fiction.

The modern writer's struggle is all too often an attempt to escape irony, because the ironic voice is too easily all-knowing or 'omniscient'. Omniscience can often sound a little weary, and risks coming over as patronizing. Radical subjectivity is one escape.

The opening line of Bellow's *Herzog* is

If I am out of my mind, thought Moses Herzog, then it's all right with me.

This isn't a first-person account; it is third-person, in the free indirect style we've discussed, but it immediately secures us inside Herzog's mind and feelings. If an ironic gap is to become visible between the external world, which has decided that the protagonist is 'out of his mind', and Herzog himself, we'll be joining him on this side of the ironic divide.

now you do it

Ironic perception

Write an ironic description of a child smelling a flower; a politician cycling to the House to make his maiden speech; or an old woman visiting her husband's grave. Remember that irony is a subversion of viewpoint. It shows us how problematic the business of knowing anything for certain really is.

Verbal irony and structural irony

It is important to distinguish between two types of irony: verbal irony and structural irony. When our man fell into the pond while fooling about and I said to him, 'You're a clever fellow, aren't you?' then that was straightforward verbal irony: the words do not mean what their surface meaning indicates; in fact they mean pretty much the opposite. Collusion is necessary between speaker and hearer to make such verbal irony effective.

Structural irony is much more complex and often not immediately self-revealing. Vladimir Nabokov's *Pale Fire* is a novel built entirely around the device of structural irony. We are given a poem written by

John Shade, and the rest of the book is an analysis of that poem by Kinbote, an analysis and exposition of Shade's poem and life by someone who, we soon come to realize, is evidently insane. This insanity takes the form of bending every conceivable meaning towards the editor's own self and obsessions. This can be seen as that 'anamorphic projection' characteristic of the paranoid vision in fiction, which is discussed on pages 153–59 in the section on fiction and paranoia.

Here we have a structural irony, since the consciousness of Kinbote is the medium through which the narrative must pass. We start to realize that this particular 'stream-of-consciousness' is far from being a neutral medium; it is tangled, torrential, weeded and murky. So now we must treat every word of the text before us with an ironic detachment. We cannot afford to be trusting. Irony demands suspicion of us as readers. The more 'structural' the irony, the more all-encompassing is the suspicion with which we must read it.

What generates suspicion? Information. If we have only one source of information, then it is harder for us to doubt it. This is why the monstrous states of the 20th century always sought to limit the sources of information to themselves. It is why foreign broadcasters were censored.

If we think about this in terms of irony and fiction, then we soon understand something about the gap that irony opens up. To doubt a report, to cast it in an ironic dimension, we must have at least one other source of information. This can be the reader's own intelligence and experience: this is the case with 'A Modest Proposal'. Our own morality

now you do it

Sharpen your pen

Use irony as a probe. For it to be effective, such an instrument always needs to be sharp. Employing something of Swift's dispassionate objectivity, write a piece in which you advance a modest proposal for stopping global warming.

Cynicism

Irony as a mechanism of defence against seriousness rapidly becomes tedious. There is a type of 'laddish' writing, which in its self-applauding cynicism debases irony to the point of uselessness. Consistent cynicism is frequently nothing but the protective carapace of the morbidly sentimental. Beneath the hard shell of the mollusc there lies a soft mush, often of self-pity. Cynicism in ironic mood will soon induce readerly narcolepsy, or if the reader remains awake at all, it might be only through irritated incredulity. Such vacuities should be avoided by the writer except for demonstrating the emotional shallowness and distended self-regard of certain fictional characters.

must know

Offsetting irony

None of us lives entirely ironically. Irony in fiction, as in life, must always be offset by something else. In Swift's case it was 'savage indignation' at the injustice and stupidity he witnessed around him in society.

breaks the trust between text and reader; we cannot accept cannibalism as a remedy for Ireland's undoubted ills.

Often the irony opens up between the different characters in the text. Let us say that a protagonist meets Dave one night; he knows him well and he likes him. Dave tells him that he has had to leave Rosie because, to be frank, the sex isn't good enough. He has appetites that Rosie simply can't fulfil. The next night our protagonist meets Rosie, of whom he is also fond. Rosie now informs him that she has had to leave Dave because of his drinking and general fecklessness. Our protagonist does not protest that this contradicts the story he heard the night before, instead he allows both versions of reality to co-exist in an ironic space in his mind.

What does the irony here consist of? The knowledge that people are always telling the stories of their lives, and that they tell them in such a way that the telling makes it possible for them to continue with those lives.

The philosopher Nietzsche remarks that if memory has a quarrel with self-regard about some incident in a person's life, self-regard has a tendency to win, and the memory is re-written until it stops being a source of shame and disgrace. This is what is happening in this ironic moment: one person believes he is leaving a woman because she cannot fulfil his requirements, while the woman believes she is leaving the man because he can't fulfil hers. Both statements can co-exist in an ironic narrative space; both might even have a certain truth to them. The writer does not need to spell anything out, or make a judgment. Irony is often most effective when it is most subtle.

Irony acknowledges the rifts between people and the fact that different versions of reality do not correspond, or add up to one coherent account of things. Different versions of the 'same reality' are contradictory, combative, embittered, fractious, at odds. Why? Because people are all those things too; that's why courts of law exist to test evidence forensically, so as to find out which versions of reality are the most convincing. Irony is an admission of the fact that all versions of life are tainted with self-interest, self-importance and the need for survival.

want to know more?

- **If you want to read a classic master of irony, read Swift.**
- **Watch Ricky Gervais's series 'The Office' or 'Extras' and think about how they achieve their effects.**
- **See the glossary on pages 183–89 for definitions of some common literary terms.**
- **Find examples of poems that use irony, such as Peter Finch's 'All I Need is Three Plums (with apologies to William Carlos Williams)' or Kenneth Koch's 'Variations on a Theme by William Carlos Williams'.**

8 Humour in fiction

We wish to be like this, but the truth is that we are otherwise. This is the essence of humour. The same fractures that we observed in irony provide us with the raw material for humour in fiction, and the main difference is one of mood and tone. Where irony, in Swift, grieves and mourns the wretched state of humanity, in Joyce or Beckett at their surreal best, it generates mirth. The fractures between our version of reality and the reality itself produces whoops of delight. In our absurdity we are seen to be funny, not because of ourselves, but despite ourselves.

Humour in fiction

What is the function of laughter? In fiction, as in life, it helps us to survive what might seem unendurable. It is a fictional tool with many purposes in the novel.

must know

TV comedy

The scripts of Galton and Simpson, particularly 'Hancock's Half Hour' and 'Porridge' represent some of the finest comedic writing of our time. Read them and learn.

Riotous assemblies

Pale Ebenezer thought it wrong to fight
But Roaring Bill (who killed him) thought it right.

Irony has brought us by a natural progress to the subject of humour in fiction. Let's start with a couplet of verse. You either find the lines of Hilaire Belloc printed above funny or you don't. If you do, there's no obligation to consider why. Analyses of humour are notoriously unamusing. Freud's *Jokes and Their Relation to the Unconscious* is probably a book as free of the prospect of laughter as any volume ever published. And yet this couplet encapsulates a fact about humour as tersely as any piece of prose writing: humour always arises out of dissonance of language, emotion, intention and register.

Ultimately all this can be summarized as the dissonance between expectation and fulfilment. Dissonant forces effect a fissure, as tectonic plates moving against one another eventually create a buckling of the terrestrial crust. Into this particular gap either a smile or a short burst of laughter intrude. Laughter can sometimes heal the fracture, by expanding the latitude of comprehension. On the other hand, as the great humourist Max Beerbohm was only too aware in his later years, it can presage murder on a substantial scale. Good torturers are usually the ones who find their work not merely well-paid but relatively amusing. Humour can be sadistic as well as healing. We should always be careful what we are doing with it in fiction.

Ebenezer has four syllables to his name, which makes him a lumbering quadruped, linguistically speaking, while Bill is a single roaring monosyllable. Bill is evidently a force of nature, and meeting the pale ponderer with his Old Testament name, and his carefully considered belief in pacifism, brings out the worst in him. It is the words here, remember, that generate the humour. The Billyness of Bill seems unsuppressible. Faced with this Ebenezer loping squarely towards him, he would be prone to violence in any case, but faced with a *pale* Ebenezer, committed to non-violence and piety too, a murder both prompt and bloody is surely Bill's only option. It would be as fatuous to blame him for this as to blame a hungry lion for eating an antelope.

Things are simply thus, and it is the thusness of things that the couplet sums up; if we smile or laugh it is because the incongruity of intention and language has conveyed to us the inevitability inherent in the confrontation. And there is a kind of justice in inevitability. That which is inevitable can't finally be questioned: such are the terms of life. Take them or leave them. William the Conqueror doesn't have to be quite as demotically lethal as Billy the Kid, but they both need to be quick on the draw if they're to maintain any kind of respect out there on the street. That's Bill's Law.

One of the classic exemplifications of such dissonance in language is the run-in between the

now you do it

Human pain

It is curious how frequently humour finds its subject in human pain. This is as true of fiction as it is of life. Write a story in which a character's pain becomes funny.

now you do it

Juxtapositions

The dissonant registers of language, the collision of the grand and the demotic, or the precise and the prattling, are the source of much fictional humour. Think of some characters you could juxtapose to comic effect.

Latinate and the Anglo-Saxon, discussed before (see page 53). Possibilities of conflict are built into the very structure of the language. The Romance words set against the Teutonic ones might register as a sort of polysyllabic grandeur encountering the humdrum vernacular.

W. C. Fields was one of the great comedic talents of our time, and it is hard to see how any seriously comic modern writer could ignore the achievements of the cinema; it might often be his starting-point. 'What a mellifluous apellation,' says W. C. Fields on hearing of Mae West's absurdly coy name. The reason the words can be deployed so deftly in this particular mouth is because of Fields' ferocious ability in an equal and opposite direction. Offered water to drink, he famously replied:

*Never drink water, my dear. Didn't you know the fishes **** in it?*

Try translating that into Latinate language and see how quickly the different modes of speech turn acids into alkali. The context of this makes it even funnier for it provides a further element of dissonance.

According to some accounts, Fields was being entertained at the time by a tee-total singer and his devoted mother. At a certain point in the evening, the mother, who lived with her son, of whom she was very proud, suggested that her beloved boy, a musical celebrity, might make his way to the piano and 'grace us with a song'. 'The only way your son could grace me,' Fields is reported to have retorted, 'is by cutting his vocal chords with a stiletto.'

It is the clash here not so much of vocabulary, for both statements are in their way genteel, as of expressed savagery meeting perfect table-manners. The more precise the language then, the greater the dissonance generated, and the more humour there is in play.

Pale Ebenezer keeps encountering Bill. In one of his films, Fields listens to a secretary admonishing her fiancé down the telephone. She reminds him of his profoundly insalubrious habits during their time together. 'You'll die by drowning in a vat of whisky,' she says, pronouncing what she evidently thinks is an unanswerable anathema. Fields turns to the camera and intones, with evident sincerity: 'O grave, where is thy victory? O death, where is thy sting?' We are looking at registers of language that are deliberately employed to go slightly out of sync with one another, and this is always a major source of humour in fiction.

The clergyman and wit Sydney Smith, on being asked if he believed in the apostolic succession (a sore point for centuries between the Roman and the Anglican faiths), replied with considerable *gravitas* that he did, of course: how else could one explain the direct line of descent between Judas Iscariot and the present Bishop of Bath and Wells? The weightiness of the theological discourse leads to the lowly clash with a grubby individual whom he happens to loathe. This is grandeur head-butted by dwarfish insolence.

It happens all the time in Shakespeare, and in Dickens. But it doesn't have to happen through personification and dialogue; it can also happen simply through language, in the precision of its

must know

The right word

Linguistic precision is indispensable to the humourist in fiction. The right word uttered at the right moment invariably trips up pretension, with delightfully catastrophic results. The greatest humourists are always avid devotees of 'word awareness', and great readers of dictionaries.

lexical and tonal discord. There is no greater exponent of this technique than Samuel Beckett. At the beginning of *Malone Dies*, the eponymous hero is anticipating his death, sooner rather than later. But he considers the possibility that he may be mistaken, and that some form of longevity may still be his. He thinks to himself that he might still survive Saint John the Baptist's Day, or possibly even the Fourteenth of July, which has its own festival of freedom. He then says 'I would not put it past me to pant on to the Transfiguration...'

now you do it

Great insults

Shakespearian insults are famously brilliant, with such examples as canker-blossom, want-wit, whining mammet, living drollery, foot-licker and whoreson malt-horse drudge. Make up ten examples of creative modern-day insults that you could use in a work of fiction.

It is surely the placing of the word pant there, in amidst the grandiloquent-sounding liturgical feasts, which announces a truly modern genius of dissonance. Never has catastrophic *miserabilism* found more caustic precisions than in some of Beckett's writings. Chaplin's clowns, in comparison, are saccharine-sweet; they don't smell foully the way Beckett's do, and they smile altogether too much. Everyone speaks precisely here, or a rebuke swiftly follows, though a rebuke might follow anyway.

It is partly a question of priorities; what is the hierarchy of significance here, and why? Where does the dissonance come from? In the great Jewish joke, two violinists on the *Titanic* decide to ignore the clamour for the life-boats and stand bravely up on the prow playing the songs that their Yiddish mothers taught them years before. 'Dark Eyes' is one of their party pieces. They play this so beautifully that they forget for a moment the extreme peril of their situation. Only when the iceberg scrapes along the hull of the ship, and looms out of the mist, does one of the musicians suddenly burst into tears. 'What are you crying about?' asks the other, in genuine astonishment: 'It's not *your* boat.'

It's funny because of the miscegenation of two different registers. It is entirely right and proper to fret a little more about the damage or loss to your own property than the damage or loss to your neighbour's. But when such a concern displaces the awareness of imminent death, the result is either tragic or funny. Sometimes in the best modern fiction, it's both at the same time.

With a writer such as Evelyn Waugh, we often encounter that possibility of malicious glee in the sounds and echoes of dissonance which so came to haunt the elderly Max Beerbohm. Waugh employs his own disenchantment with reality to generate not grief but laughter; he wielded his own unashamed malice forensically.

One day he records in his diary that Randolph Churchill has been admitted to hospital. He says he's going for exploratory surgery then the surgeon discovers a tumour. The tumour is subsequently discovered to be non-malignant, and removed. What a miracle of modern science, Waugh muses to himself, in the privacy of his own pages: to find the one bit of Randolph that isn't malignant, and then take it out.

The dissonance is so simple that one's laughter has a kind of innocence to it. A very technical term in a medical sense is translated into a more universal form of description, to approach the all-too-easily-detestable Randolph. This is the technique of Waugh's fiction being rehearsed in his daily observations.

now you do it

Only joking

What is a joke? It is a celebration of the split between intention and reality, or between appearance and reality. It acknowledges the same rifts as irony, but in celebratory mood. Think of a funny story you've heard that achieves this effect, and write it as wittily as you can.

now you do it

Regional humour

People of different cultures, even different geographical areas, have individual ways of laughing at themselves. Explore the differences you might find between a Glaswegian joke, a Liverpudlian joke, a Welsh joke and a Home Counties joke.

Humour and pain

Humour is never neutral and it is very seldom entirely innocent. The writer cannot hide behind the cant phrase 'It's only a joke'. Writers must take responsibility for how they generate laughter and why. Here we might return to Freud. Freud believed that jokes were the sites of psychic distress and collusion; that the dissonance they registered was also a conflict elided, and his favourite example of this was an old Jewish story (see below).

Even in our jokes we try to bury our passions; desire and hatred are only ever just beneath the

The rabbi and his wife

An eminent rabbi taught at a yeshiva. He was far from wealthy, but his great learning made him an object of devotion in the local community. He married a very beautiful young woman. To earn a little money they took in lodgers. One of these was a handsome but severely disturbed student. So disturbed was he that on certain days he couldn't accompany his teacher to the school. After one such occasion, the old man returned home to find the handsome student kissing his beautiful young wife with some passion. He remonstrated with them both, and the wife protested: 'But you know he only does it because he's sick in the head.' 'If he's so sick in the head,' said the old rabbi, 'why doesn't he just kiss the stove?'

surface. Fiction permits them some release, but it can be a perilous procedure.

Freud believed that we reveal ourselves in jokes; the comic fiction writer effectively says that we reveal ourselves through the medium of his humour. He portrays us in our self-estimation, by showing how askew that estimation really is when confronted with reality. He shows the ill-married relationship between the image in the mirror and the image in the mirror of our minds. Out of this vertiginous gap he pulls gag after gag.

But we should never forget Freud's warning about the significance of humour: it is often the site of vulnerability. The man who never stops jesting about sex might well be disguising something inside him which he'd rather conceal. We have to think carefully about humour, as we do about any other aspects of fiction.

want to know more?

- **Both Samuel Beckett and the James Joyce of *Ulysses* were true masters of the modern humorous mode. Read them and learn.**
- **W.C. Fields was also a great writer of comedy, although it appeared on film. Watch him in *My Little Chickadee*, *It's a Gift* or *The Old Fashioned Way*.**
- **Also listen carefully to whoever the person in the corner is who always seems to have a group of people standing around laughing. Analyze the way in which they are producing their humour. Is it self-deprecating? Word play? Anecdotal?**
- **Just as comedians keep a book of gags, fiction writers should note any funny things they overhear that might come in handy one day.**

9 Themes, motifs and modes

This chapter will explore different routes into fiction. These are not so much forms as modes. There are different 'ways of seeing' in writing which produce radically different fiction out of the same materials. Fiction re-arranges reality; myth is part of reality. When fiction returns to myth or history, it does something different to the mythographers and historians: it is opening up spaces for itself to work in.

Themes, motifs and modes

Fiction can come from anywhere: your home town, a chance visit, two hours spent in the library, or a lifetime's engagement with myth or history.

must know

Using myth

To return upon myth, the modern writer must make that myth come alive. It must be perceived, approached and evoked from a 'modern' angle; otherwise the writing will be merely pastiche. If as a writer you want to use a myth, you must find a way of living inside it. You must make myths come alive, and you must make them your own. Otherwise they will always seem second-hand.

The return upon myth

The word mythology is an interesting one, combining the Greek word for story – *mythos* – with that for reason – *logos*. By the time we can call something mythological it has already lost some of its mythiness; we are already distancing ourselves from it, studying it, analyzing it, examining its component parts.

We moderns are at the end of the tradition, not the beginning. This is the condition known by the American critic Harold Bloom as *belatedness*. We are the Johnny-Come-Latelies of the storyline. All our myths are subject to the forensic study that we call mythology. We can't adopt a pose of innocence. If we do adopt such a pose, so late in history and culture and art, it's not innocence we'll actually achieve, but kitsch.

What we are equally likely to do is to return upon myth by way of irony. James Thurber re-tells the story of Little Red Riding Hood. Everything happens as before, except for one significant difference. When the wolf pretends to be the grandmother, having eaten the old woman and climbed into her clothes and her bed, he merely prompts Little Red Riding Hood to take a gun out of her pocket and shoot him dead. Thurber's moral is simple: wolves don't really look much like your grandmother, and it's not as easy to fool little girls as it used to be. That's a classic ironic return upon myth and legend.

James Joyce was one of the great modern humorists, and also one of the greatest users of myth. Modern writers have returned to mythic themes, not simply to recapitulate them, but to explore their hidden meanings, turn them into allegories, render their truths psychological, make them ironic or point up hidden assumptions which the original authors could never have considered. They also return there for sources of energy, often of a chaotic and unpredictable nature. Myth was a patterning device for a writer like Joyce, but also an endless source of anarchic celebration.

Let us think for a moment about *Ulysses*. What is it that Joyce is actually doing here? His example has been followed so many times in subsequent writing that it is worth a little study. It is a good opportunity to ask ourselves why modern writers have become so preoccupied with myth.

Myths are the first great stories we tell about ourselves and the world. Myths make sense of the heavens, explain the recurrence of seasons and the growth of plants, explore creation and confront the fact of death. In other words, they address the greatest realities that confront our human condition. They do this with a ruthless imaginative thrust, and with such a daring and facility for connecting up the disparate portions of reality, that the figurings and patternings still astound us.

The constraints of civilization, the repression we live with as the price of modern civility, do not apply here. Gods metamorphose into animals and impregnate goddesses, warriors slaughter their

now you do it

Re-analyze

Choose a novel you have read and enjoyed. Re-read it, paying attention to the techniques the author used to introduce character and theme, speed up or slow down the pace. Work out why the story affected you. Which mythic pattern does it fit into?

fellows with relish, girls turn into weeping trees, snakes speak a language that is both cunning and beautiful, even though the words are announcing the wreckage of Paradise.

In returning to myth we are in one sense returning to ourselves; to a primal energy we sometimes seem to be losing. Myth shapes reality around the human spirit and the human body. And in myth the old Doctrine of Signatures (which holds that God marked everything He created with signs or signatures) applies: everything connects up with everything else. The great chain of being has no missing links. It is then, in the broadest sense, a type of fiction, since the word fiction comes from the Latin word *fingere*, which means both to shape and to fashion, but also to feign.

T. S. Eliot reviewed *Ulysses* in 1923 and thought that what Joyce had done was to find a principle of ordering the chaotic nature of modern reality by borrowing myths from antiquity and using them to structure contemporary experience. Eliot over-estimated Joyce's reliance on myth for purposes of ordering, and under-estimated his use of it as a source of energy and irrepressible delight. One of the constant astonishments of myth is its unpredictability. This is not a mechanical version of reality, which might be one reason it has such an attraction for a mechanical age.

Joyce did use the sections of Homer's *Odyssey* as a structuring principle for his great novel, but the structuring freed him. It gave him his plot, and permitted the coincidence of the ancient and the modern, allowing for an ironic space to open up between the two. The irony at the immediate level is the contrast between the heroic exploits of Ulysses and the less heroic activities of his modern-day incarnation, Leopold Bloom. And yet were this kind of contrast one-dimensionally the case, the novel would be much less of an achievement than it actually is, because the more interesting fact is that Bloom is heroic in his way. He is cuckolded by his wife and intimidated by the anti-Semitism he finds around him in Dublin; professionally he is something of a non-entity; he has even been unfathered by the loss of his son, and yet somehow he embodies the human genius for warmth and love and creativity. He is not ultimately being satirized by his author, but celebrated.

Elizabeth Cook in her remarkable *Achilles* also takes the writings of Homer as her starting-point. The story of Achilles is well-known. He was the son of the mortal Peleus and the sea-nymph Thetis. During the Trojan War, Achilles was the greatest warrior of the Greeks. In the *Iliad,* we witness the great fighter's terrible anger. He falls out with his commander Agamemnon after the latter takes his rightful human booty, a girl named Briseis. As he stays in his tent, the Greek troops are driven back towards their ships. Achilles has a beloved companion, Patroclus, who dons Achilles' armour and goes out to fight Hector, son of King Priam, in his place. He is killed. Achilles then decides to abandon his feud with Agamemnon and fight Hector himself. He kills him and in his continuing fury drags his body behind his chariot. Only once he has satisfied his rage does he finally allow Priam to be given back Hector's body for burial.

Later writers added to the story. Achilles' mother, the nymph Thetis, dipped him in the Styx so he might be immune from any human damage; but she missed a tiny portion of his heel, hence his vulnerability, and the phrase 'Achilles' heel'. To prevent him being killed, he was hidden at Scyros and disguised as a girl while recruitment was going on for the Trojan War, but he ended up going anyway.

These are the basic materials of the 'story'; what Elizabeth Cook does to turn it into our 'plot' is to inhabit Achilles imaginatively. We have already seen how archetypal plots tend to move inwards in the modern age; how a topographic descent in Dante or Virgil becomes a psychological journey in modernity. While Cook retains the literal truth of her sources, she psychologizes Achilles. We explore the interior of his spirit in a way that was of no interest to Homer. He, unlike us, did not live in the age of psychology. Cook also manages to recover some of the astonishing energy of the original in her narrative; her language finds the speed and unexpectedness we look for in myth. She has succeeded in achieving what the contemporary mythic writer aims for: to find a modern language that permits the expression of the original mythic energy.

Writer as Reader

Neither James Joyce's *Ulysses* nor Elizabeth Cook's *Achilles* could have been written without astute acts of reading. The good writer is always a good reader, and any writing genius is also a reading genius. This does not mean the writer will have read everything; far from it. But what is read will be transmuted into writing. Creative reading is an inseparable part of the process of creative writing. Let us take a look at this process.

Shakespeare read books with an intellectual avidity that immediately internalized them; they became a part of him. He was honeycombed with his reading, and we can see some of it re-emerging through his own writings: Ovid, Plutarch, Livy, Holinshed's *Chronicles*, Chapman's *Homer*, Florio's *Montaigne*. And always traversing all the plays and poems like a mighty braid, the English Bible.

Two and a half centuries later, Herman Melville is writing *Moby Dick* and simultaneously reading Shakespeare. Shakespeare on the page astonishes him, sufficiently so that he can write in one of his letters: 'If another Messiah ever comes 'twill be in Shakespeare's person.' He is fascinated by the 'dark characters' in the

Elizabethan's plays. At this point Ahab begins to form in Melville's mind, though he was not there in his first conception. In other words, and this is crucial, the reading of Shakespeare generates the portrayal of Ahab, and it does something else, too: the riot of metaphor, the breathtaking cross-fertilization of language that characterizes *Moby Dick* is connected by a direct lineage to Melville's reading of Shakespeare. The richness of linguistic invention that makes Shakespeare's writing so promiscuously creative finds a posthumous life in Melville's writing, just as Ovid and Homer did in Shakespeare's. Reading resurrects the work of the dead in the writing of the living.

It isn't just Shakespeare who helps to form Ahab; Milton's Satan is in there too, along with Melville's reading about Napoleon. The point is this: Ahab was as much read into existence as written into it. This quintessential epitome of fanaticism and single-mindedness, this man 'with a crucifixion in his face', this dark focus of fascination, is the weird and wonderful offspring of energetic and exploratory reading. He would not exist without it. Reading by a writer has brought him into being.

All writers should train themselves to read with the same intelligence and resourcefulness that Shakespeare read Ovid, Elizabeth Cook read Homer, or Melville read Shakespeare. Reading with such intensity is not a passive process; it germinates the mind and seeds the page. A story like Angela Carter's 'Overture and Incidental Music for *A Midsummer Night's Dream*' is a perfect example of the way a writer seizes upon literature for her own purposes. She then re-creates it.

must know

History

We live in history; we are historical creatures. The historical tense is the one in which most fiction is written. History is, in one sense, fiction's natural subject. History provides fiction with its credibility; its 'specific gravity'.

Fiction and history

If one major resource of the contemporary fiction writer is myth, another is history.

What do we mean by historical fiction? If we were to be strict, then presumably no character could appear in the text without a historical warrant. That is very seldom the case in fiction though, any more than it was usually the case in Shakespeare's 'history plays'. Actual 'historical' characters usually mingle with fictional inventions. This can cause trouble, and is in fact designed to cause trouble, since the trouble here is a necessary part of the excitement.

The American novelist E. L. Doctorow is a classic instance. He started out by revisiting the Western for his first book *Welcome to Hard Times*. This was by way of limbering up. He then took on the American spies the Rosenbergs, and their trial and execution, with *The Book of Daniel*, before setting about the mighty themes of 20th-century celebrity, adventure and injustice in *Ragtime*, which featured such actual luminaries of the time as Harry Houdini, Emma Goldman and J. P. Morgan. These historical characters were effectively ventriloquized by Doctorow, a procedure that made some queasy. They had encounters for which there was no historical documentation; they said things no one ever recorded them saying. And even more importantly, they met people they could not have met in their actual lives, because Doctorow had just invented them in his book. The novelist has defended his practice as a way of writing bigger fiction than many of his contemporaries, and frequently invokes Tolstoy as a forebear. When he wrote about gangsterism in *Billy Bathgate*, much of it was based on the actual gangster Dutch Schultz.

So what is going on here? Fiction is what is going on. And we can perhaps see this more clearly with a little more historical perspective.

We might ask, for example, what is going on in *Middlemarch*? There, all the characters are invented, but they exist in a recognizable historical time – the mid-19th century in England, in the centre of England, hence the name of the town Middlemarch. George Eliot (or Marian Evans, which was her real name) came from the Midlands; she knew about the centre of England. She was fascinated by the scientific, technological and intellectual developments of her time.

Although her novel is not normally referred to as a 'historical novel', it is undoubtedly a novel full of history. The farmers are battling with the same agricultural conditions that beset actual farmers at the time; the doctors with the same diseases and social problems regarding public hygiene. The characters are extrapolated out of history; their specific gravity comes from our sense of their entanglement in the mesh of actuality that is 19th-century England. Invention is in a permanent conversation with actual history, and it is this that gives the characters their strong feeling of documentary reality.

Jill Dawson in *Wild Boy* takes something from recorded history, in this case the material surrounding the Wild Boy of Aveyron, the feral child who was discovered in France in the 18th century. In fact, nobody was ever to find out where he came from or why he ended up living in the woods. The

now you do it

Clarifying setting

When you write in a historical setting, you must introduce it with clarity and efficiency. Consider the following opening sentences and the ways in which they convey information.

- **'He was called Smith. Which, in itself, was a marvel; for it seemed as if the smallpox, the consumption, brain-fever, gaol-fever and even the hangman's rope had given him a wide berth for fear of catching something.'**
- **'It was 1947 when Mutt and I was married. I was singing in Happy's Café around on Delaware Street.'**
- **'It was a bright, cold day in April and the clocks were striking thirteen.'**

Look for other examples and then write half a dozen opening sentences of your own that effectively set a story in a particular period.

must know

Researching history

Historical research must be used with passion. The fictional writer must live inside history to write it, just as Elizabeth Cook lived inside the myth of Achilles, or John Gardner lived inside the mind of Grendel.

power of Dawson's narrative comes not from the bare historical facts, but the inventive speculation that her skill as a fiction writer permits her.

Her plot explores the possibility that Victor, as the boy was named, had been thrown out of a family because he had some behavioural problems; that the gash around his neck had been a bungled attempt to kill him; that his real salvation came not from Dr Itard, the specialist in deafness assigned to his case, but Madame Guérin, the woman who spent the rest of her days caring for him. Victor was to be taught to speak, but he never did, though he could mimic certain words.

This raises interesting questions about socialization, and what happens to a child who is not brought up in a linguistic community, but it also raises another question about Victor: was it possible that he suffered from some sort of autism, since autistic children sometimes do not communicate linguistically at all? Jill Dawson tells us in a poignant afterword that her own son is autistic.

This book is a very good place for a writer to go to find out how to use history intelligently in fiction. *Wild Boy* uses history as the spring-board for its own reflections. The historical factor is a goad to intelligent invention. The author takes what history gives, but does not permit herself to be limited by it. History knows almost nothing of Madame Guérin, but Dawson brings her so vividly to life that we end up as convinced of her 'character' as we are of Victor's and Dr Itard's.

Good historical writing requires either an immersion in the period being evoked, or a remarkable degree of inventiveness or, even better, both. Alfred Duggan never wrote a historical novel set later than the 13th century. He said this cut down on research, since people very seldom had the foggiest notion what had really gone on in the societies he portrayed. His historical dialogue always seems very convincing, partly because he always speaks in contemporary idiom. This is not a bad strategy.

We might ask what the difference is between historical fiction and a highly intelligent, stylistically impressive journey into history like Lytton Strachey's *Eminent Victorians.* What different thing is being done? The phrases 'imaginative freedom' and 'invented structures' might cover it, and somewhere inside those two phrases, fiction and psychology meet and create convincing characterization.

And the effect of this meeting can probably be seen nowhere more powerfully than in Michael Moorcock's *Pyat Quartet*. This astonishing evocation of the 20th century, over a vast geographical and political range, has as its central character Maxim Arturovitch Pyat, born on the first day of the century - or maybe not. One of the elements that Moorcock endlessly examines and re-examines here is the function of memory, and the relationship of memory to need. And wherever we find need, he tells us, we will also find prejudice. Perhaps the only indisputable thing Pyat ever tells us about himself is 'My own memory is a confused one.'

Moorcock is an enormously accomplished writer in many different modes and he pulls off something here that a lesser writer simply could not manage. He brings the great and scandalous characters of the age on-stage; he portrays them through the

must know

Pastiche

Pastiche dialogue is frequently embarrassing. Once a writer starts littering the page with *thees* and *thous* and ampersands, the ghost of Errol Flynn can soon be seen striding the battlements. We already know it's set in the past; no need to remind us every time someone opens his mouth.

rambling, pernicious, profoundly unreliable memorializings of the old rogue Pyat, now reduced to a life of relative peace and tranquillity in London's Westbourne Grove. Hitler is here and Mussolini, and too many other historical horrors and scoundrels to catalogue. We never know when we can believe him, and yet enough believable history keeps intruding into the text to convince us that some portion of what he tells us must be true. In a continuing act of inverted anti-Semitism, he constantly denies his own (at least partly) Jewish origins. History and deception have become inseparable in him, and a part of the function of the quartet is to force us to ponder how 'making a story' is of its very nature a type of deception. 'Fiction' remember comes from the Latin word for shaping, *fingere*; in shaping something into a narrative we must to some degree deform it. And *fingere* also meant 'to feign'.

The astonishing pace and gusto of Moorcock's books is only made possible by his mastery of all those fictional and linguistic skills we spoke of before. When he is in full swing, he is a writer of Shakespearean vitality and range.

Fiction and place

We have already said that we live after Einstein, and therefore must acknowledge that to every 'where' there is a 'when'. There is also a recent type of writing, sometimes described as 'visionary topography', which insists with equal vehemence that for every 'who' there is a 'where'. Place is identity; the landscape outside the human skull always shapes and fashions the psychological landscape within it.

Place in writing has often been connected with travel. Certain writers seemed to need to move around the world, filling their notebooks, as a form of fictional stimulus. One thinks of Graham Greene, Evelyn Waugh or Paul Theroux. It's hard to imagine a writer like V. S. Naipaul always staying in the same place; he would be a different phenomenon entirely. But there has always been another sort of writer, for whom rootedness in a specific place provides the necessary fictional material. George Mackay Brown is a classic instance of this. His native Orkney constituted the entire world of his writing, and that writing took its strength from the intensity of his rootedness in location and tradition.

At the head of our new group of 'visionary topographers' we could place Iain Sinclair, though there are others too, such as Nicholas Royle. Sinclair reads all history and human dynamism through the specificities of place, and that place is usually (though not always) London. In such a realm, of course, the competition is fierce. Many great writers have lived in the metropolis and written about it. Dickens is here an inescapable presence. The evocation of London in a novel like *Bleak House* remains unforgettable. At the beginning, the way that fog obscures the river is described with a potency that comes from living with the phenomenon and studying it at close quarters. When he describes the operations of the law and its grandiose headquarters in London, he shows us how vividly he writes in terms of place; he is always a potently visual writer:

This is the Court of Chancery; which has its decaying houses and its blighted lands in every shire; which has its worn-out lunatic in every madhouse, and its dead in every churchyard; which has its ruined suitor, with his slipshod heels and threadbare dress, borrowing and begging, through the round of every man's acquaintance...

This is a writer who thinks in images, and the images are all rooted in place. Sinclair is, if anything, even more rooted in place, particularly his chosen habitation, London. Sinclair as a writer can be hard to classify; it is sometimes difficult to know what sort of text it is we're reading: history, topography, occult meditation, a phenomenology of the modern city? His metier

now you do it

Travelling back in time

Each place is full of history. An examination of place will involve an examination of time, and that involves an imaginative journey backwards. Find some old family photographs from when you were a child. Describe the places in which they were taken in as much detail as you can remember.

is really the hybrid form. A book like *Downriver* is simply unclassifiable, though by that very fact it perhaps fits Bakhtin's notion of the restlessness of form that characterizes 'the novel'. Sinclair sees the city as a palimpsest, an endlessly overwritten site of its own history, its building, re-building, self-defence and ultimately its self-demolition. Sinclair's relationship to the city is a mixture of love and hatred. He watches with dismay the ceaseless proliferation of Cyclops lenses, as surveillance CCTV cameras make London the most observed tract of land in the world.

But the great metropolis is an obsessive spur to Sinclair's imagination, and the way he *reads* the city is its main interest here, whether he is re-exploring the Whitechapel Murders, or trying to fathom how the London Orbital circumscribes London, the way Blake said Reason was always the outer circumference of Energy.

Sinclair's writing is a classic instance of defamiliarization. He defamiliarizes a familiar environment by decoding its traces with an unexpected intensity. He uses maps, photographs, old texts (particularly architectural and occult ones), memories, history, and his own epic walks, to portray the present reality of London with a vividness that is never less than arresting. The city is for him a permanent synchronic reality, which is to say that the past is ever-present. It's all there; it just needs finding. Sinclair stakes out the city like the scene of a crime, the way Walter Benjamin said Atget had photographed the streets of Paris. His fascination with the urban labyrinth is exemplary.

Regional novels

When the region from which the writer comes is itself foregrounded, then some critics have spoken of the 'regional novel', though there is perhaps a hint of condescension in that phrase. Nobody talks about Sinclair writing 'regional novels' when he writes about London. But the fact is that a writer can come to believe that her or his 'region' lacks credible representation, and one form that representation can take is fiction.

This is what happened with writers such as John Braine, David Storey, Stanley Barstow, Alan Sillitoe and Barry Hines. Legendary titles were created and subsequently made into films. Their characters still hover about in the imagination: *Room at the Top, This Sporting Life, A Kind of Loving, The Loneliness of the Long Distance Runner, Saturday Night and Sunday Morning, Kes.*

In all these books we feel that a type of life was being revealed that had not fully entered the world of the novel before: a northern, working-class life, something only seen before from the windows of stylistically social superiors. And the same process goes on now with a writer such as Jonathan Coe and the Birmingham that provides so much of the material for his work.

must know

Capturing particulars

The life in each place is specific. People live not in generalities but specifically. They have a particular way of living, speaking, working, eating, drinking. The fiction writer has a certain responsibility not to be a mere tourist, gathering data.

Coincidence

The mention of synchronicity gives us the opportunity to talk about coincidence in fictional writing. It's not possible to plot without confronting the issue of coincidence.

At the beginning of Evelyn Waugh's novel *Scoop*, John Courteney Boot, a fashionable novelist, asks Mrs Algernon Stitch, a society lady, to help spirit him abroad. He is in profoundly low spirits as a result of a liaison with an American *femme fatale* who has already driven a number of British men like himself into the asylum. There is at present a crisis going on in the mythical African country of Ishmaelia. Mrs Stitch is lunching that day with Lord Copper, proprietor of *The Daily Beast*. Boot and Mrs Stitch between them hit upon a plan. Mrs Stitch will talk up Boot's credentials as a writer of renown to the newspaper owner, and see if it is possible to get John sent to Ishamaelia as the best man to cover the forthcoming war.

Lord Copper is duly charmed, and on his return to Fleet Street demands of his staff that his newspaper must have Boot. The bemused staff, hardened newsmen one and all, are not given to reading fancily written contemporary novels, and therefore have not the faintest notion who Boot might be. They check their files only to find that there is indeed a Boot on the staff of *The Beast*, one William Boot, Countryman, who writes the following kind of sentence:

Feather-footed through the plashy fen passes the questing vole...

He is summoned to London, and somehow press-ganged into taking the Ishmaelia job, although all he truly wants to do is return home to Boot Magna Hall, there to observe his beloved rodents and ferns.

On such an inherent improbability is based the whole plot of the book. It permits the insertion of an innocent into the cynical world of journalism. William Boot's uncankered eye acts as a defamiliarizing device, which can look upon the outrageous goings-on all about him with a benign wonder. As if this spectacular 'coincidence' were not enough, the wrong Boot is also sent out to report on an incident in which Mrs Stitch's car has ended up at the bottom of the steps leading to a public urinal.

This is a particularly blatant example of the use of coincidence, and yet the device itself is never far away from fictional plotting. If Waugh, in characteristic fashion, exploits inherent improbabilities for comic effect, others employ the inherent improbability that is coincidence for radically different purposes. In *O How the Wheel Becomes It*, Anthony Powell brings together people from different times and places by the same initiating device, if more 'realistically' deployed.

The writer Geoffrey Shadbold is presented, in his role as reader and editor for a London publisher, with a diary, the diary of someone with whom he was once connected, a person he greatly disliked. More to the point, the two men had once competed for the affections of a flighty young woman. Through this unpublished manuscript, and the connections it facilitates, the entire plot will be fashioned. The effects will turn out to be predictably ruinous. Now in a sense that particular manuscript landing on that particular writer's desk was a coincidence, a contrivance that facilitates all the connections that the plot will need.

We could stop to think for a moment about what we actually mean by the word 'coincidence'. Two or more things happen in a way that appears to defy the normal laws of probability. That is coincidence, and once we put the matter this way we realize that it is inseparable from any form of plotting in fiction. In *Oedipus Rex*, we have to accept the extraordinary improbability that Oedipus has an argument at a crossroads with an unknown man and kills him, with no notion that this man is his father. He then proceeds to Thebes and marries an unknown woman, Jocasta, who turns out to be his mother. This is coincidence on the grand, indeed the mythic, scale. It is fateful coincidence of the sort that brings catastrophe in its wake.

These are comic and tragic possibilities, but the realistic mode of plotting exploits coincidence too – otherwise it can't bring everything together within the delimited space of a plot. In Andrew Crumey's *Mobius Dick*, for example, a man and a woman at a university happen to sit down at the same canteen table. They both put their books down, ready to read. One is called *Quantum Fields in Curved Space*; the other Thomas Mann's *Doctor Faustus*. They start to talk to each other. The subject of one of Mann's other books arises; this is *The Magic Mountain*, a novel about a man who went to a tuberculosis clinic in the Swiss Alps. Ringer, the scientist, points out that this is an extraordinary coincidence, because the book he is reading is about the Schrödinger equation, the fundamental rule of quantum mechanics. And Schrödinger made his discovery while recovering in a tuberculosis clinic in the Swiss Alps.

must know

Beware

Coincidence is unavoidable in fiction, but an excess of it will soon provoke incredulity. It must be treated with caution and should never simply be a cheap way to resolve a dilemma with the plot.

And so begins the plot of the book: with a striking coincidence. The rest of the novel is to some extent a meditation on coincidence, on how similarities and parallels co-exist within any given space; how modern physics makes laws out of coincidence.

We tend only to mention coincidence in plotting if we believe it to be too overt. In other words, if it appears to lack verisimilitude. If it is exploited for comic purposes, as in *Scoop*, we simply delight in it. If it is convincingly portrayed as the motor of a narrative, as in *Mobius Dick*, then it appears to be an acceptable device for fiction to employ. The truth is that we barely notice it if we are reading a well-written narrative and are absorbed in its created world. For example, in Kurt Vonnegut's *Mother Night* the protagonist, Howard W. Campbell Jr, who broadcast for the Nazis during the war (by prior arrangement with the American government) finds himself living in an apartment block in New York. An old woman there recognizes his voice; she was a Jewish internee in a concentration camp and had listened to the broadcasts. Now how likely is this? If we are asking this question, then we have to add, do we mean 'likely' inside or outside fiction, since they are not necessarily the same thing. Fiction creates its own world of 'likelihood', and this depends to a considerable degree on the genre of the writing.

Many of us now find the endings of some of Dickens's novels hard to bear because of their over-resolved nature; the sense that coincidence and natural justice must conspire to overcome all frustration, all injustice, all happenstance that promotes unhappiness. Serendipity appears to have taken over from reality.

What in fact is serendipity? It is the fortuitous good fortune which appears to contradict our normal expectations of life. The word was coined by Horace Walpole in the 18th century. He was thinking of a story, 'The Three Princes of Serendip' (present-day Ceylon), who, whenever they venture forth, are showered with unanticipated blessings. The end of a novel by Dickens presents us with a world turned suddenly serendipitous, at least for the deserving. The bad ones, of course, go to whatever appalling fate properly awaits them.

So we might think that modern fiction, with its gritty determination to confront the dark side of

now you do it

Questions to ask

Ask the following questions of any piece of writing, whether your own or others'.

- **Is the characterization original and rounded?**
- **Is the language fresh, lively and unclichéd?**
- **Does it work on its own terms? For example, if there is some mystery, does the author make you interested and lead you to the unravelment? If there is a created world, do you believe in it? Are the relationships plausible?**
- **Is it straightforward and one-dimensional or are there layers of meaning?**
- **Does it grab your interest and maintain it?**

must know

Serendipity

Serendipity can be delightful. Too much of it though will become syrupy, and syrup on any page of fiction tends to make things sticky.

reality, might eschew serendipity. Magic Realism often exploits it for its own purposes though, and there is one remarkable work of contemporary fiction that is effectively an analysis of the theme of serendipity. This is David Mitchell's *Ghostwritten.*

Ghostwritten actually has a cult-leader called Lord Serendipity, who directs a poison-gas attack on the Tokyo Underground at the beginning of the book. He then might or might not appear in various incarnations throughout the rest of the novel. Whether he does or doesn't, the principle of serendipity itself is the essential structuring device of Mitchell's fiction here.

Gossamer threads of connection tie one web of existence to another, with momentous results. One man pushes a woman out of the way of an oncoming car and changes everything that subsequently happens in the book, even though they never have anything further to do with one another, and had never met before. Someone dials a wrong number, and by making a shop-assistant go back into a shop to take the call, changes that person's life for ever, because as a result of delaying his departure he then meets the love of his life.

Mitchell almost seems to taunt the reader with improbabilities, but at the same time he is foregrounding the device of coincidence on which so much fiction is constructed. He is in one sense letting us see how fiction works.

Coincidence can never be used innocently by the modern writer. If we are in Magic Realist mode and exploiting all the fabular possibilities of that type of writing, then we can't pretend it's the hard-nosed detective realism of Raymond Chandler. Much coincidence will also require a large enough structure to contain it. Mitchell constructs such a spacious structure in *Ghostwritten*, but a short story in a realist mode in which three extreme improbabilities occurred would be in danger of becoming inherently ridiculous.

Jorge Luis Borges used his stories as spaces in which to explore logical and philosophical possibilities, and yet he always anchored his meditations in a verisimilitude that is appropriate to them. He found the details that prevented the intellectual games from simply floating away, losing the 'specific gravity' that any work of fiction always needs. But Borges was one of the most knowing of writers, and also one of the most learned. He is a hard act to follow. Better to admire and do differently.

must know

Intensity

In a drama of confinement, character begins to express itself with considerable intensity. It is this intensity that the writing will exploit.

Fiction and the drama of confinement

Think how often a fictional situation is presented to us as a drama of confinement. On the television the likeliest scene is an interrogation room. A man sits behind a table; another man on the other side is attempting to get the truth out of him, to find out if the child is still alive, and if so where she has been locked away. We are here witnessing a gladiatorial encounter. This has its sports version in a game of snooker or a tennis match. Two wills and two intelligences meet, confront each other, attempt to outwit one another, see who will break first. We look on, fascinated.

Dramas of confinement present us with humanity pressed to its extremes of endurance. We like to witness such situations.

now you do it

Use the senses

Write your own drama of confinement. Consider the details that will make the claustrophobia of the setting vivid for your readers, using the senses (sight, smell, touch, taste, hearing) as appropriate.

The setting of this scene of confinement can be anywhere. It can be an island, as it is in *Robinson Crusoe* or *Lord of the Flies*. It can be a hospital, as it is in Thomas Mann's *Magic Mountain* or Solzhenitzyn's *Cancer Ward*. It can be a prison as it is in *One Day in the Life of Ivan Denisovich*. It can be the inside of someone's skin, as it is in John Gardner's *Grendel*.

Here the monster taken from the Old English epic *Beowulf* is endowed with enormous intelligence, more intelligence than most of the men he confronts, but he is excluded for ever from the company of men, because he is shaggy-haired and repellent: even he cannot abide his own appearance. And his mother is even worse; she entirely disgusts him with her rudimentary table manners. He cannot join the company of men, so he kills them instead, after analyzing them closely.

He is a moveable intelligence unit, and a sniper. We live with him inside the pelt of his confinement and share his bitter reflections.

Such situations of confinement provide many writers with their essential scenario. Think of the function of the ship in the writings of Melville and Conrad. Men can't escape from it during the voyage without drowning, and so inexorably they discover one another's identities, sometimes with good effects, and sometimes with dreadful consequences.

Think of this as a rudimentary template for the drama of confinement:

A lift disburdens itself of most of its passengers at Floor Five. There are only two people left inside. Before it can reach the next floor, the lift breaks down. The older man looks at the younger woman and sighs. But the woman stares at the man intently. After a moment, she says, 'You don't remember me, do you?'

Any number of consequences could follow.

Fiction and displacement

A great deal of defamiliarization in fiction comes from displacement; this is often a displacement in location or time, but there are other types too, and these usually take the form of a reconfiguring of our five senses. We were talking in the previous section about dramas of confinement. Two of the examples given there are classic instances of displacement in fiction: *Robinson Crusoe* and *Lord of the Flies*. In both cases people are taken away from the normal rules and expectations of society, to an island where they must survive as best they can.

When Thomas More wrote *Utopia*, providing us with the name we have used ever since, he employed this device. If you shift your characters in this manner, then all of their normal preconceptions might be challenged. They might, for example, start to wonder why we think so highly of gold – not a useful element on an island if you are trying to work out how to survive. So why would people kill one another to acquire it? Displacement allows for the re-assessment of prejudices and preconceptions.

In the instances we've mentioned, the displacement is a literal one – there is a place at the heart of the word dis*place*ment, and we have been removed from it, to somewhere strange and unpredictable. The foundations of our life are thereby put into question. This is still a classic device of adventure fiction and cinema. The plane crash or

now you do it

Unpredictability

Fiction often moves us from our accustomed habitation. This can be external, from place to place, or internal, from certainty to something more unpredictable. One of the classic age-old plots can be summed up as 'stranger comes to town'. Try writing a story of displacement on this theme (although it need not take place in a town).

the shipwreck deliver our fates to a new place, stripped of our normal expectations.

SF and displacement

Now think of what goes on in classic SF writing. Here we have more complex, even more elusive, displacements. *Gulliver's Travels* is one of the founding texts of SF. In *Robinson Crusoe* we are transported elsewhere, but the normal rules of perception continue to apply; reality has grown lonelier, but it hasn't re-arranged itself entirely. But think of Lemuel Gulliver in Lilliput and Brobdingnag. Here reality *has* re-arranged itself. In one place Gulliver becomes a giant surrounded by tiny people; this gives him a different vantage-point on reality. Perception has been radically re-routed. Gulliver is looking through a telescope at reality. Then in Brobdingnag it is he who is the midget, gazing up at the monsters all about him. His vision has become a microscope. He sees with vivid detail the coarse details of the life all around him, and it is grotesque:

The Kingdom is much pestered with Flies in Summer; and these odious Insects, each of them as big as a Dunstable Lark, hardly gave me any Rest while I sat at Dinner, with their continual Humming and Buzzing about mine Ears. They would sometimes alight upon my Victuals, and leave their loathsome Excrement or Spawn behind, which to me was very visible, although not to the Natives of that Country, whose large Opticks were not so acute as mine in viewing smaller Objects.

Good SF writers keep their eye on what is going on in the world of science and technology; often they have a training in science, like Isaac Asimov or Arthur C. Clark. The fact is that the passage above simply could not have been written without the publication of Robert Hooke's *Micrographia*, with its superb illustrations of the large grey drone-fly and the flea. When Pepys collected his copy of this book soon after its publication in 1665, he sat up until two in the morning reading it, and described it as 'the most ingenious book that ever I read in my life.' Gulliver's eye in Lilliput is a telescope, and in Brobdingnag it is a microscope, and much pain it causes him as he gazes upon the human body. The most famous of the illustrations in *Micrographia* had been a sixteen-inch fold-out of a louse.

The genius of *Gulliver's Travels* was to understand that perception had been altered for ever by the introduction of the telescope and the microscope, and to make use of this in fiction.

So what developments in science and technology might an SF writer use in a similar manner today? Let us take a look at this opening:

The Röntgen Reader sat in the train carriage and tried to concentrate on his book, Telekinetic Waves. *He had opened it at the chapter entitled 'The Diffraction Patterns of Melancholia'. But he couldn't read. He could sense the woman opposite directing her energy at him. He didn't want to receive it; he really didn't want to read her, not today. He'd had relationships with women, none of which had lasted longer than six months. He was tired of reading women. He was here to escape, both women and the people in Washington. The train rolled through the darkness. Then he registered the figure at the back in the white raincoat. The minute he saw his face, he felt the message coming through: 'We really do need to talk to you, Brother Tom. I've come all this way to talk to you.' An official Communicator then. There was no escape, he'd always known there wouldn't be. He turned back now and stared at the woman. Her lips didn't move but he could read the words coming out of her mind: 'My husband doesn't touch me any more. I need a little love. Women need a little love. Why do you look so different?' Because I cannot speak and I cannot hear, thought Brother Tom; because I am deaf, dumb and a Röntgen Reader.*

Because I can read everything that is in your heart, and you can read nothing that is in mine. And because they use me to kill people. When he stepped off the train the man in the white raincoat followed.

must know

Writing about science

Science is one of the great unexplored areas for modern fiction to exploit. Its riches have hardly been touched yet.

All SF and futuristic writing provides us with early clues as to the nature of the displacement we are about to undergo. On the first page of George Orwell's *Nineteen Eighty-four*, the clock is striking thirteen (see box page 125). Time itself has changed. It has gone ahead of itself. But then who decided to divide time up into units of twelve in the first place? (It was the Babylonians, in fact, and decimalizers from Napoleon on have been fighting a battle against those cumbersome and unwieldy numbers.)

So what clues are we being given in the opening passage above? A Röntgen Reader: this sounds like a literary device, but one that should alert us to what is going on. Röntgen was the man who invented (or discovered) the X-ray, which was for a while known as a Röntgen-Ray. So if we have a Röntgen Reader, then what is it that he can see through, the way that an X-ray penetrates the flesh to see the shapes beneath? He can read minds, it seems; he is deaf and dumb, but from his position in his world of silence he can read minds. So this displacement is one of perception, since the other details (the train, the man from Washington) seem to indicate that we are in the present.

At the beginning of William Gibson's *Neuromancer*, we are presented with a fictional situation we know well. A man moves through mean streets, surrounded it seems by enemies. He needs to protect himself; he's not sure who's out to get him or why. He's smart but exhausted. He needs a weapon. It could be the beginning of a novel by Raymond Chandler. But the language alerts us to something else; it displaces our normal expectations with a terminology we've not encountered before. This man rents 'a coffin' to sleep in. A local warlord is protected by his 'joeboys'. A woman, an assassin it seems, has retractable switch-blades that come out of her nails. 'Nerve-splicing', it seems, is a medical procedure that re-arranges your nervous system and repairs the shattered nerves that are all too common in this world.

And most famously of all we find 'cyberspace', a term invented by Gibson in this novel, one that the world has happily accepted as designating that area of virtual reality where electronic communications are conducted. The displacement here is both dystopian (conjuring a reality even worse than our own) and conceptual; we find ourselves accepting a set of ideas and functions, which operate only in this fictional world.

now you do it

Thwart the hero

Write a story set in the future, the past or any unfamiliar world, using a classic formula. Take a protagonist who wants something badly and wants it now, then thwart him or her. Obstacles can be introduced by one or more anti-heroes, and they should get worse as the story progresses. Start the suspense on the first page and choose a quirky main character.

Fiction and science

Given that we live in the age of science, science itself is probably the most under-used resource in modern fiction. The inventive use of genuine scientific thought has largely emigrated to genre writing, like SF, which partly explains the enormous popularity of much SF writing today. We have already seen how a writer like Kurt Vonnegut complains that because of his 'SF classification' he is not taken as seriously as he might be by some people. What the classification does allow him, however, is the freedom to speculate, often at length, about our scientific understanding of the world.

The lack of the use of science outside SF is something of a puzzle. The writer Ian McEwan is famously devoted to the work of Darwin, and does sometimes use Darwinist conceptions in his work. Similarly Thomas Pynchon has spent a writerly lifetime obsessed by the Second Law of Thermodynamics (the Law of Entropy) and the work of the 19th-century physicist James Clerk Maxwell. In his novel *The Crying of Lot 49*, there is even a stamp featuring Maxwell's features; this is effectively used as a diagnostic test to find out if someone has special powers of perception, or not. In both instances here though, the science being used is over a century old.

Part of the problem is the sheer difficulty of understanding much modern science. Lawrence Durrell claimed that the inter-relationship of the texts in his *Alexandria Quartet* was ultimately based on Einstein's Theory of Relativity. Most readers would probably have to conclude that the fiction could have got along nicely without the science. Modern physics after the quantum revolution of the 1920s produces a certain nervousness in the modern fiction writer, even though the subject itself continues to fascinate the reading public, hence the ceaseless proliferation of explanatory accounts of modern science for non-scientists.

John Banville, a writer of immense scope and power, took on both Copernicus and Kepler in two separate novels. They are both narratives of the 'fictionalized life' variety, and both work remarkably well.

The advantage of writing about scientists from centuries ago, of course, is that the subject – scientifically speaking – is closed. We are at a sufficient distance now from these figures to be able to place them in a historical context.

Mobius Dick by Andrew Crumey is an example of a modern novel that takes on the quantum world of physics and actually does something with it. The book is partly a meditation on

The Periodic Table

Primo Levi wrote a remarkable book called *The Periodic Table*. This is usually classified as fiction, but it is in fact a classic instance of Bakhtin's remarks about the hybrid character of fiction; how it is always re-inventing itself in forms that seem to defy classification. Primo Levi was a chemist, and he was also a concentration camp internee during the Second World War. He takes Mendelyeev's periodic table, which classifies the elements according to their atomic numbers, and transfers the whole taxonomic system to humanity. So we have a constant movement back and forth between the characteristics of the elements, whether they are active or inert, their isolation or readiness to marry other elements promiscuously, and the characteristics of people whom Levi actually knows or has heard or read about. It is a beautiful example of how scientific knowledge and intelligence can actually inform fiction; can provide it with new shapes in which it might think itself out in an original manner.

how identity is implicated in the apparatus of its own observation; or to put the matter differently, how we 'are' what we are 'seen to be'. The great Danish physicist Niels Bohr put it thus: 'The apparatus must be seen as part of the phenomenon.' Crumey makes ample use of Schrödinger's thought experiment about the cat, which either is or isn't dead depending on the moment of its observation. This summary makes it sounds as though the novel could be schematic, but in fact as a piece of fiction, it is an exhilarating thought-experiment in its own right.

It is a tragedy that more fiction writers don't explore the possibilities that the modern world of science affords, because when they do, the results are often startlingly unexpected.

must know

Oddballs

Great scientists are usually fascinating. They can be seriously odd too – Newton certainly was. If you can prove that you have mastered the basic science, then scientists are a great subject for fiction.

In 2003, Clare Dudman published a novel entitled *Wegener's Jigsaw*. The subject is in effect how the discipline of modern geography took the shape it did; now that surely sounds like a textbook way of having your book turned down by a publisher before a single page has ever been read. In fact *Wegener's Jigsaw* is an extraordinary novel, utterly compelling, and a perfect candidate for showing how modern scientific thought, if the writer can become inward enough with it, yields unexpected riches.

Wegener was a fascinating man, who led a fascinating life. The material provided by his expeditions and his terrible experience of war provide the writer with unparalleled narrative possibilities, as intriguing as any found by Banville in his accounts of the lives of Copernicus and Kepler. In constant counterpoint to the narrative excitements is the developing theory of 'continental drift'. This is 'intellectual fiction' in the best sense, and its raw material was the development of modern science.

Fiction and religion

In *The Devils*, Dostoyevsky portrays the character Stavrogin, who has decided to find out how much his entire person might approximate to evil.
The novel is an exploration of how much our metaphysical notions of the absolutes of goodness and its opposite can in fact be incarnated in human form. In Thomas Mann's *Doctor Faustus*, the modern composer Adrian Leverkühn accepts evil, a form of diabolic intelligence, as the price of his achievement in the arts. This is a meditation on evil in politics as well as culture, and has for its background the rise of Nazism in Germany.

In Jeremy Leven's extraordinary book *Satan: A Case Study*, the satanic becomes a metaphor for manipulative intelligence, for an intelligence so separated from any ethical consideration that it might be designated 'evil'. It can also be separated entirely from any biological casing, leading to some interesting considerations about 'non-human intelligence' and cybernetics. Some fictional returns upon the theme place a certain ironic distance between ourselves and the originary theological matter. Books such as *I, Lucifer* by Glen Duncan and *Satan Wants Me* by Robert Irwin have, as a sub-plot, the possibility of Old Nick getting to put his side of the story at last – often with hilarious results. This is not new: William Blake believed that Milton's problem with *Paradise Lost* was that he was of the devil's party, 'without knowing it'.

There is also the remarkable novel by Mikhail Bulgakov, *The Master and Margarita*, in which the Devil turns up in Moscow during Stalin's reign. Here the satanic presence is used for primarily satirical purposes. This novel, written in great peril at the time, probably contains the most hopeful remark ever made about the writing of fiction by one of its practitioners: 'Manuscripts don't burn'.

And there has been throughout all this a type of religious writing in fiction, which we could call 'experiential'; evocations of those who live a particular sort of life, in religious communities or simply with religious beliefs. It was a tenet first of the Enlightenment, then of modern political thought, that religion would quietly die out, as the progress of scientific method in the realm of thought marched steadily on. Something like the opposite appears to be the case.

must know

Serious subjects

All humanity was religious once. The French poet Charles Baudelaire insisted that there were only three serious subjects for writers: sex, religion and death. But religion as a subject in fiction should never be treated lightly; it is the core of too many people's lives.

now you do it

In depth

Re-write a story from a religion with which you are familiar, making it vivid and contemporary. Remember that religion in fiction must be explored from the inside, or it will be merely two-dimensional.

A majority of people in the United States insist that the Book of Genesis gives some kind of 'literal' account of creation; if this is bad science, it also displays bad reading habits, because Genesis is not that kind of writing, and was never meant to be. What all this does bring home, however, is the continuing significance of religion as a theme for the fiction writer. This significance seems unlikely to wane in the near future.

This then raises a question: how can this potent subject be approached by the fiction writer? It might seem evident to say it, but the statement should be made none the less: it can't be approached through ignorance. If the 'religious believer' is merely the Other, the stranger, the alien, then a type of thin satire might be produced, but nothing more profound. If the figures kneeling in church, or rocking back and forth at the Wailing Wall, or taking their shoes off to enter the mosque, are seen entirely from the outside, their use in fiction will make for thin gruel.

In *A Portrait of the Artist*, Joyce shows us Stephen Dedalus as he considers the possibility of becoming a priest. The great sense of election, the troubled consideration of sin, the sense of being separated from the world in an elevated transaction with the Almighty, all these are powerfully evoked, and the reason they can be so powerfully evoked is because Joyce knew such experiences from the inside.

But he then did something unexpected. In *Ulysses* he creates Leopold Bloom, a Jew, and in creating him he invents something like a modern Falstaff, a celebrator of life who is not entirely dignified. This required something that the portrayal of Stephen

Dedalus did not: an attentiveness to the Other, until the Other loses something of that otherness, and starts to become an intimate acquaintance of the imagination. This is one of the greatest achievements of which fiction is capable.

There is a sort of feminine counterpart to Joyce's portrait: *Going In* by Jenny Newman. Without any of the stylistic pyrotechnics for which Joyce is rightly famed, *Going In* is a quietly intense account of that female election which consists of becoming a nun. Brigid Murray, having left her Liverpool home for a French convent, effectively undergoes on a personal basis the crisis that the Catholic Church itself was undergoing globally at the time: the conflict between the spiritual requirement for obedience and the personal need for emotional fulfilment and intellectual honesty. It is a tribute to the book's honesty that no easy answer is ever offered to this dilemma, because there isn't one. (The author re-approached the theme in another book, where the motif of entry into religious life was reversed into the theme of exit from it.)

The book does what all good fiction should do, however: make it that much harder for us to simplify people. The characters in *Going In* have a reality in all their emotional, psychological and intellectual complexity, which is entirely compelling.

now you do it

Character study

When trying to introduce depth into a character, use the following exercise.
1. Write a sketch of them as you see them.
2. Write a sketch of them as they would see themselves.
3. Describe a character that is the opposite of the one you described in point 1.
4. Describe a character that is the opposite of the one in point 2.
5. Look at the four descriptions and underline the parts you find interesting. Amalgamate them.

Fiction and psychology

We keep speaking about psychological observations and explorations in fiction. What exactly do we mean? There is hardly ever any technical psychology going on; we don't for example usually analyze the precise movements of a character's psychological machinery, though David Foster Wallace does in fact use this device for ironic purposes in stories such as 'The Depressed Person' in *Brief Interviews With Hideous Men*. The different texts contained in this book are grouped together as 'short stories' but this is a fiction in itself, a convenience for booksellers and reviewers. There are monologues, interviews, pathological reports. Once again we are reminded of Bakhtin's insistence on the hybridity of fictional forms. In fact, like Melville, Wallace can't see a literary form without immediately setting out to dismantle it, or to expand it to the point where its previously perceived parameters have become effectively residual.

The language of this story has about it an apparent objectivity, a clinical terminology, that leads us at first to assume that it is a report on the depressed person. It is only the way certain perceptions are conveyed, how they are squeezed by the narrative, which leads us to realize that this is indeed a report, but one compiled by the depressed person herself. It is an account distorted by the very distortions it is meant to be analyzing, or as Karl Kraus once put it, the symptom here imagines it is the cure. It is effectively a forensic account of the device of the unreliable narrator, and it is all explored in terms of psychology.

It becomes apparent after a few pages that 'the depressed person' has come to inhabit a clinical universe; her very mode of thinking about herself and everyone around her is expressed in clinical terms. Everything is conceived and described in relation to her own depression, and what gradually becomes apparent is that this clinically descriptive prose is in fact not forensic, but monomaniacal. The occasional expletive that finds its way into the supposedly neutral judgments is the nearest 'the depressed person' ever comes to humanity.

As an exemplification of how an internalized language of pseudo-scientific gravitas can be as damaging as it is liberating, Wallace's text is often Swiftian in its rancour, and it is a rancour directly generated by the study of psychology.

More often in fiction the psychology is presented as part of the action, as an aspect of characterization. When Starbuck in *Moby Dick* pleads with the crew to continue whaling purely as a commercial enterprise, simply as a way of making a living, they ignore him. Already they have been beguiled by Ahab's mission, and the secret society in pursuit of the white whale. Melville provides us with a wonderful example of the portrayal of communal psychology in fiction (it is also, incidentally, a perfect example of the drama of confinement, and its implications for those who would dissent).

It is part of our modern pattern of thought to have become convinced that, whereas in earlier times psychology was seen as the expression of personality, in ours it is often seen as the language of a personality's confusion or fragmentation. We don't think we're in charge of our minds and their functioning, anything like as much as we would like to be, and this explains our constant employment of the term 'the unconscious'.

Take this opening passage of a hypothetical novel:

Father came back from the Front with his body intact but his mind in ruins. After mother would finally coax him to sleep, it would begin. Rats crawled through the mud of his dream, making for his face. Then he would wake screaming. I would wake too. Over there he had sung every night:

Take me back over the sea
Where the alleymen can't shoot at me
Oh my, I don't want to die
I want to go home

But now he was home, and he'd brought the Somme with him. I was ten years old, and I was at the Somme too. Out there in the darkness where men screamed. I could taste the mud too.

must know

Gesture

Psychology in fiction usually expresses itself in gesture. The subtlest gestures can sometimes be the most potent. Think of six examples from your own reading.

The psychology here is indistinguishable from the history that prompted it, as it often is. The fictional device (how horrors once endured refuse to be repressed, and return to haunt us in our sleep) was used to unsurpassed effect by Shakespeare in *Macbeth*, when Lady Macbeth sleepwalks and re-capitulates the murder of Duncan.

We examined earlier how there is something 'unspeakable' about the quality of much modern experience, and this is what the passage above is exploring: the reality can't be 'spoken'; it can't be 'told'. At the beginning of D. H. Lawrence's *Lady Chatterley's Lover* we see how the war has ruined much of European civilization and has physically devastated one man, Clifford Chatterley. His physical state is indistinguishable from his psychological state. Lady Chatterley cannot find her own identity, her own meaningful psychology, without a meaningful relationship with a man, which Clifford can now no longer provide. So Mellors the gamekeeper provides it instead. He has managed to remain a little less ruined by the war.

Imagine a story called 'Tennis'. It is set in Wimbledon during the quarter-finals. Two young women are battling it out on Centre Court. In one of the special boxes sit two people: one is one of the young women's mother, and the other her fiancé. We never watch the tennis; the narrative directs us instead to the reactions of the two people in the box, we see the tennis match through their perceptions. It starts to become apparent that the ecstatic reaction of the mother every time her daughter hits a winner is never matched in the features of the fiancé. Similarly, whenever the daughter loses a point, the anguish in the mother's face is not reflected at all in the young man's, who seems either expressionless or almost smiling.

Then the narrative draws our attention to something else. The young man spends more time looking at his fiancée's opponent than he does at his betrothed. And we gather (from hearing the man's thoughts?) that the young star from Italy has a stunning physique. If one of the two tennis players were to be the candidate for some glamour shots in a glossy magazine, no one would be in any doubt which one would be more likely to have the cameras pointing at her. When the battle is finally won, and the tennis player's mother leaps up from her seat in delight, the fiancé remains seated, and simply puts on his sunglasses.

What has happened here is that psychology has been revealed, several psychologies in fact, through gesture and expression. This is showing rather than telling, in terms of psychology. And it is often the best way to convey it.

Fiction and paranoia

In discussing modern fiction and psychology, it is not possible to avoid the term 'paranoia'. There is even a 'school' of modern writing known as 'paranoid fiction'. We have discussed some of these texts previously. Important writers are involved here, so let us try to see why this is such a significant area for modern fiction.

In Holbein's painting *The Ambassadors* in the National Gallery in London there is a distorted skull at the foot of the canvas. In one sense this is not 'in' the picture at all: it is what is known as an

now you do it

Endings

Most people can recall several examples of memorable opening sentences, but how many memorable endings can you think of? Endings recapitulate the main motifs, even if they cannot tie up all the parts of every narrative. Think of the endings you have found potent and satisfying and ask yourself why.

'anamorphic projection' and can only be seen if the viewer moves over to one side of the picture and stares skew-whiff along it. To see the skull you have to stop seeing the rest of the painting clearly; and if you are seeing the rest of the painting clearly then you cannot see the skull. You see either the living beings or the emblem of their forthcoming death, but you cannot see both simultaneously. The ambassadors and the skull are not viewable without a change of visionary angle. This is a perfect image for understanding the paranoid vision.

David Swanson, in his book *The Paranoid,* characterized paranoia as being constituted by the following characteristics.

- A projection outwards on to the world of self-criticism.
- A conviction of the hostility of exterior reality towards the subject.
- A profound suspicion of the world and its intent, often resulting in the discovery of elaborate schemes of esoteric malice.
- A marked conviction of the centrality of the subject.
- Systematic, and frequently plausible, delusions.
- The great fear of having one's own autonomy constantly undermined.
- An inflated and deformed sense of self-worth, exacerbated by a sense of imputed inferiority.

This sounds like Grendel in John Gardner's novel; but then it also sounds like Lee Harvey Oswald in Don de Lillo's *Libra,* and it sounds like any number of people in Thomas Pynchon's *The Crying of Lot 49*. Paranoiacs make wonderful fictional subjects because they make complete sense of their world, even if they are forced to do so by a process of anamorphic projection.

Grendel might well turn out to have been a far more influential text than is often acknowledged. It achieved a particular tone that has been much imitated since, though seldom matched by the same consistency of hostile estrangement, a lexicon and a syntax of disenchantment. By grafting the human consciousness of isolation and alienation on to the inhuman subjectivity of Grendel, an entirely cogent and entirely belligerent view of humanity is facilitated. Grendel combines the instinctive potency of a non-linguistic creature with all the world-weariness of a highly sophisticated linguistic one. This optic provides an unblinking meditation upon the self-serving, self-deceiving, self-mythologizing ways of men. This narrative need never be compromised by charity. We are always seeing the skull here, but like a revenant from an emblem book, it howls.

Grendel is a philosopher in his flinty isolationism; he is a solipsist of bestiality and a poet of natural devastation. He thinks of himself at one point as 'an ugly god pitifully dying in a tree'. The allegorized paranoiac who is Grendel permits a high degree of defamiliarization, that distancing and alienating optic that we saw Swift employ so startlingly in *Gulliver's Travels*. Everything that might be seen in standard perspective is viewed instead through the anamorphic projection.

The core of the paranoiac vision in modern fiction is that the 'official version of reality' is not merely wrong, but pernicious. It is designed to deceive us, to keep us from the truth. Such a version of reality appeals to a great many people; hence the immense popularity of *The X-Files*.

Let us return to Thomas Pynchon, since he is a founding figure in this type of writing. *The Crying of Lot 49* can be read as an allegory of paranoia. The narrative reveals a secret society, held together by codes and cryptic assignations, and through the gradual revelation of this invisible fraternity the oppressive features of the greater society are made manifest.

Oedipa Maas, the book's heroine (though no more heroic a heroine than Leopold Bloom in *Ulysses* was a hero) comes to assemble in her mind the significance of the secret society of

must know

Unresolved

The natural impulse of fiction is to make everything link up. The truth is that everything in life does not link up - some things remain unexplained and disconnected. This degree of contingency, of unconnectedness, needs to be acknowledged in realistic fiction writing or it will seem over-contrived.

the Tristero from the fragmentary clues she is given. There is the possibility here of what we called earlier 'structural irony', since the Tristero are either a group of rebels which a system of total control in society has engendered, or they are the symptoms of Oedipa's increasingly frenetic mental collapse.

The book's ambiguity leaves open either reading. What the Tristero represent, assuming that they have a reality outside Oedipa's mind, is the need to win back the basic terms of communication from a state that has seized them in its entirety. The Tristero represent, even embody, a form of communication outside the control of the state. They are epistolary bandits. They have their own system for delivering mail secretly. In discovering what they mean Oedipa comes to understand for the first time what the society to which they are opposed really means. She learns at last to read: to read the society around her, and its real significance.

We discussed earlier the relationship between causality and contingency, how one is the realm of law and the other the realm of possibility. There is an ongoing transaction between them in all fiction. But in the paranoid vision there is no contingency; everything must finally be translated into the realm of causality. What appears to be an accident isn't. It only seems so because we do not yet have enough information to see the causality behind the apparent contingency.

In Don De Lillo's *Running Dog*, the sought-for pornographic film of Hitler operates thematically as emblematic of the pornographic pull that the subject of Nazism exerts on our present-day media. It is as though the dark secret of history was here to be revealed, in the demonstrably, nakedly human aspects of history's most sought-after demonic. It is as though there is a secret interior to humanity's chronicle, a kernel of esoterica, and an inverse grail quest might lead us at last to discover all the arcana of villainy.

DeLillo's fiction exemplifies a strand in American culture that might be described less as post-war, post-Bomb or post-modernist, than as post-Dallas. The killing of JFK, and the widespread incredulity at the conclusions of the Warren Commission, have probably fuelled the paranoid element in American life as much as the perception of the internecine politics of the Vietnam War (although much of the mood was anticipated in that intriguing book and film, *The Manchurian Candidate*). The inheritance is there not only in films such as Oliver Stone's *JFK*, which deals directly with the subject, but also in others such as Francis Ford Coppola's *The Conversation*, which feed upon the general sense of state-organized deception.

Paranoid culture gorges on the notion that those in power are mired in mendacity, and the greater their resources the more all-pervasive their lies are likely to be. DeLillo himself tackled that theme in *Libra*, a book that is simultaneously a study and a product of the paranoid strain in modern writing. In *Mao II* the writer portrayed is so bitterly estranged from the reality that is his subject, that when he re-enters it, it promptly kills him. It was only his Howard Hughes-style paranoid reclusiveness that had allowed him to go on living at all.

It soon becomes apparent that in finding parallels between certain forms of modern fictional writing

must know

The quest for meaning

The theme of much modern fiction is the quest for meaning. Underlying the plot is the firm notion that everything can be explained, if only we can discover the code in which the meaning is hidden.

must know

Paranoia

Exploration of 'the paranoid vision' is dependent on the writer's own genuine passion. If the use of this mode is merely a contrivance, an artificial device, it will tend to become rapidly alienating if employed at length.

and paranoia the problem is not so much searching for what to include as deciding on what to leave out, and how far back to go. Some texts are easy. *The Ordeal of Gilbert Pinfold*, for example, is an entirely logical paranoid book in that it merely personifies and apotheosizes the complex of prejudices that constituted Evelyn Waugh. His own hatreds at last break free and gain a kind of autonomy. They turn on him and he merely records their speeches.

In *Hadrian VII* Frederick Rolfe explored his own paranoia as a spoiled priest, which at least permitted him to avenge himself upon the church that had terminated his clerical ambitions; he fictionally re-invents himself as Pope.

It might be possible that we already witnessed the beginning of 'paranoid fiction' in *Moby Dick*. For Ahab, the world has become a white whale; it must be crossed and re-crossed until that shape, like the sculpture hidden in Michelangelo's white marble, emerges. This obsessiveness, this persecuted and persecutory spirit, redeems Ahab from the mere utility of slaughter. The unanswerability of his passion makes him the whale's equal and finally, as the great white shape descends into its formless habitat with its one-legged captive, he ends up as the white monster's mate.

Ahab's lethal romance with the whale is a celebrated mourning for his wound; his fascination is with the world as a hole into which the whale has disappeared. He is a man, says Melville, with 'a crucifixion in his face'. The ocean is a constantly shifting hole, a hole forever filled in by tides and observation, and forever capable of rendering forth the longed-for object of desire and loathing. He is then a classic paranoiac, and his vision (however anamorphic) makes sense of everything.

At its best the paranoid stance becomes an aggressive principle of discovery. It *will* get to know the truth, as Oedipa Maas perhaps begins to discover towards the end of *The Crying of Lot 49*, however great the odds might seem against the revelation. At stake ultimately is the question whether or not there is something hidden, whether or not the paranoid stance justifies the energy it must expend to make its discovery.

In *Totem and Taboo*, Freud writes: 'It might be maintained ... that a paranoid delusion is a caricature of a philosophical system.' The same urge exists in both to make sense of the world, to find connections where others have found none.

Fiction and selection

Let us end by reminding ourselves where we started. What is fiction? It is the effective evocation of character, incident, place and time by means of prose narrative. The final 'setting' of everything is on the page. That is where writing ultimately has to work. Our fundamental resources are vocabulary, syntax and punctuation. That's where it all begins, and in this instance, in our beginning is also our end. Which is why it might be appropriate finally to address the question of fiction and selection. What do we choose to write, and why?

There is a tiny little parable by Borges called 'On Exactitude in Science'. It describes an empire so devoted to the precisions of cartography that it ends up producing a map of the land that coincides point-for-point with the land itself. It is exactly the same

must know

Selection

Selection is writing: what we leave out and what we put in define the narrative. All selected details should be telling – ultimately they constitute the information which forms the fictional world.

size as the empire. It is the supreme representation, and therefore entirely useless. Why? Because representations to be effective must select: include certain facts, exclude others.

Think of how a map works: it simplifies the data so that we can derive the information we need. If it is a road map, then all other topographic realities are subjugated to the visibility of the highways and byways, whose bright colours will stand out contrastingly from the complex realities all around them. If the map is a geological map, it will look very different indeed. The roads will disappear and in their place will be representations of the mineral content of the earth. In cartography, the principle of selection is based upon function, and it is exactly the same in fiction.

The map that coincides with the land has ceased to be a usable map; it has become instead a form of idolatry. Borges tackled the same subject from a different direction in a story called 'Funes, His Memory'. Funes remembers everything. Indeed, he can't do anything other than remember everything; he does not have the facility of forgetting, which when we think about it is a form of selection. The result is as catastrophic as the vast map of the empire: Funes is paralyzed by the overload of information with which his memory weighs him down.

Nietzsche once wrote an essay called 'The Use and Abuse of History', in which he said that any society that becomes entirely obsessed with its own past, incapable in other words of forgetting, also becomes incapable of action. The impossibility of selection would also mean the impossibility of fiction.

All these parables are pointing us in one direction: in writing, selection is everything. How we begin, which details we choose, what characterization occurs, what incident is described; all this gives the narrative its identity. Choice is shaping, and fiction as we remember comes from the word *fingere*, to shape. If we don't choose, then we are not representing situations, we are merely replicating data; this is the procedure that Borges was

An exercise in archetypes

We have already looked at universal patterns and archetypes. Understanding the function of each character within the story can help the writer to use them fully and determine whether they are pulling their weight. The main character can gather aspects from each archetype and learn from them on his/her journey. Look at the following archetypes and decide which psychological role they would play and their dramatic function in a story.

Hero
Mentor
Shapeshifter
Trickster
Herald
Allies
Shadow
Threshold guardian

Not every story will have all of them, of course. Consider some favourite novels and see how many archetypes you can identify. Write your own descriptions of characters who might fulfill each role.

satirizing. Both of his short stories can be seen as parodies of a certain fantastic dream of 'realism', in which all the facts can be included. All the facts can never be included; selection is always unavoidable. If we included all the facts, then our map would be the same size as the country, and our novel would go on for ever.

The first revelation we have of the selection process is of course the opening. Many books open with a philosophical remark that sets the tone for what is to come. The opening of Tolstoy's *Anna Karenina* tells us how all happy families tend to be happy in the same way, whereas unhappy ones are all distinctive in their misery. That gives us some notion of what is about to follow. Look at this narrative opening, and see how the selection of statements and the emphases give us vital information about what is to follow:

People mythologise. They tell a lot of fancy lies. They prefer talk to silence, even the most eloquent silence. You can't blame them. Life, without a myth, is punitive. Though sometimes it can be punitive with one, too, as we're about to see.

Someone will evidently be devoted to their own mythology, and someone will probably come a cropper; that seems to be the message, and it will probably be proved right. Selection has told us this.

It is also selection which to a considerable degree dictates the type of writing we are reading. If we wanted to describe Salman Rushdie's story 'The Prophet's Hair' as 'Magic Realism', it is partly because of the selection of detail and images. Rushdie brilliantly employs the legendary language of *The Thousand and One Nights*, but to his own narrative purposes. Such a language has a legendary quality, even allowing Rushdie to get away with apparent cliché, in phrases like 'dark as ink'. It all feels natural and controlled. The motif is the traditional one of the intolerable gift, like the gift of Shakespeare's memory in the story by Borges.

The prophet's hair is the magical gift that curses all in its path, even as it appears to bestow power. Detail, and therefore selection, is used here with genius. We are informed at one point that the

now you do it

Take note

Eavesdrop on a conversation. Listen to the way people seldom answer each other directly but manoeuvre to steer the conversation back to their own agenda. Take discreet notes.

criminal, displaying the authentic sadism of the genuine fairy-tale, had crippled his sons at birth, so as to guarantee them their lifelong income as beggars. So the crippling was by way of a patrimony; it was a form of kindliness. It was this inescapable flash of cruelty that Hans Christian Andersen also understood to be fundamental to the legendary tale.

So when we say that Magic Realism is a movement in modern writing that has opted to escape the rigours of traditional realism by tapping into fairy-tale, legend, hagiography and supernaturalism, we are to a large degree talking about its 'principles of selection'. The type of data and the sorts of images it employs alert us to the nature of the writing on the page before us.

As writers we select our form, our mode and our tone. If we elect to defamiliarize our descriptions in the manner of the Magic Realists, by surreal metaphor and simile, by factual descriptions of seemingly supernatural events, then we must ensure that the narrative form can contain such brightly lit language without losing the attention of the reader. If, on the other hand, we wish to incorporate a mass of historical research, then we must make sure that this material is deployed throughout the text in such a manner that it does not sink the narrative. If we are returning upon myths, then we must take hold of those myths with a vigour that ensures the reader does not merely feel as though old material is being re-cycled.

The manner and the matter are in endless dialogue, as are form and content. It is the writer's responsibility to ensure that each page negotiates this relationship with intelligence and tact.

want to know more?

- **Psychology is interior geography. Mapping it is an unavoidable aspect of fiction. Attending to the speech and silence of those around you every day is the usual form of research for the serious writer.**
- ***Myth* by Laurence Coupe is a truly excellent account of how modern writers have used myth and mythic archetypes for creative purposes.**
- **Local libraries are filled with archives, which are a quarry for the attentive and intelligent writer. Don't ignore what is nearest to hand.**
- **All orthodox religious narratives have a counter-narrative. These are often called 'apocryphal', which is another way of saying they have not been authorized by the official tradition. Check them out. Register the vivid imagery of these dissenting traditions, which are often of substantial use to the writer.**

10 Some practicalities

The first chair a carpenter makes often falls over: so, that is not the best one to put in the show-room window. Good writing comes through hard work and revision. Nobody's experience is important in and of itself, not in writing. The experience only becomes interesting because the writing is interesting. Robert Graves always said that the writer's best friend was the waste-paper basket...

Some practicalities

Good writing is always well-revised writing. Hardly any writer manages in a first draft to find the perfect words that end up being printed.

must know

Ask yourself

Can it be improved? Yes. Always. So improve it. Each word can be put in question. Every item of vocabulary, each syntactic rhythm: every punctuation mark. Is there a better alternative?

Don't rush: drafting and re-drafting

Writing is a process of thought in its own right. Nobody works it all out in the mind before simply writing it down; the process of writing is the work's way of finding itself, its way of coming into being. Fiction negotiates its own form as it goes along. Thinking here takes place on the page.

For this reason, rushed writing will seldom be much good. It hasn't re-thought itself; it hasn't properly discovered all of its own dimensions.

Keep re-writing until you get there.

Altering as you go or at the end?

So how do you plan and revise? Should you plan the whole book before you begin or simply get going? Should you revise each chapter as you finish it, or draft the whole thing with some urgency, and then begin the patient business of revision? Should you 'read it out', either to yourself or others? How should a writer best revise their work, by over-writing on the screen or creating a duplicate text, while preserving the original?

And another question soon arises, which can be of equal importance: when do you show your work to other people? How do you know when it is finished?

We need to be clear here: there are no rules. The only rule is what works best for you. But we can examine a few examples, and think about a number of ways of doing things.

must know

Re-drafting

Sometimes writing the first draft is the easiest part; sometimes the hardest. It depends on the writer and the book. Most good writers do a lot of re-writing. The extent to which the original is 'saved' or 'discarded' is up to the individual. One thing though is certain: a lack of scrupulous re-drafting will almost invariably mean that the finished work is not as good as it might have been.

Word processing

Most writers now work on a word processor, if not immediately, then very soon after. This has had an incalculable effect upon our working practices, if not necessarily on the end result. Think for a moment of the famous 'manuscript collections' that are stored in libraries, museums and universities. Why are they so valuable? Because they show us the working practices of writers from the past. If a manuscript has been written in ink or pencil and then revised, corrected, crossed-out and re-written, the traces remain. The same is true of a typescript corrected by hand. But if you work on a word processor, and revise by deletion and correction, then the finished text is free of any such evidence. It is free of the tell-tale marks for everyone else, but it is free of them for the writer as well. This is the most hygienic form of correction ever invented, but it does have its consequent perils.

Don DeLillo still writes on a typewriter, and he retains each version of every page that he types. Why? Because he says he does not know until the end which version will turn out to be the best. In the process of writing he is too close to the work to make a final judgment.

This is worth thinking about for a moment. Often the process of correction can produce a rush of efficiency, a wish to 'clean the text up'; sometimes even a kind of impatience with your own stylistic peculiarities. After all, if you have spent a long time in the writing, there comes a point when you wish to

now you do it

Be your own reader

When you have finished a draft, leave it for as long as possible before you return. The Latin poet Horace recommended ten years, but that is not always practicable. When you read it again, read it as though you are someone else, someone who knows nothing of your own cares and preoccupations. Will anyone really be interested? If not, try to find a way of making them so. Make the words live on the page.

have the work finalized, and ready to go out into the world. The effects of this can be admirable: lack of sentimentality, ruthlessness with compositional dither, anger at one's own ineptitudes. But it can sometimes produce over-pruning. You as a writer can cut something that was actually of value, but you might not know at the time. Is there a way round this?

One simple technique, used by many writers, is this: draft the whole book in its original form and save it as a file, then copy that file as *Filename2* and do all your corrections on this version. That leaves the original as a resource to be returned to. If you intend to explore a fundamental alteration to a major part of the text, then copy that as *Filename3*. This way you lose nothing of whatever section of work you have done. This procedure can, if necessary, be followed chapter by chapter. It is, however, much easier to see alterations on a marked-up printed page than on two separately printed sheets, but at least you have lost nothing.

This still does not answer the question as to when the revising should happen. Most writers revise as they go along, endlessly. They then produce at least one 'final' overall revision before handing the book to someone else. This, if we think about it for a moment, is inevitable. If you have made a false move with a character, then you must revise that mistake before moving on, or it will distort the whole book.

Individual corrections of words, sentences, paragraphs, can be done at any time, even amidst distractions. But that final revision, the overall one, needs some time and concentration. It should ideally come after there has been a break from the writing, and it should allow the writer enough intellectual space to see the book as a whole. It is often only at this point that one can sense misdirections, false notes, unwanted diversions, longeurs. By this time some of these might well have been pointed out by others.

must know

Readers

Only show your work to people you have a reason to trust. Egotism or carelessness in a reader can have a devastating effect on the writer mid-way through the work. On the other hand, every writer needs critical readers to point out areas that aren't working. If you choose three or more readers you can trust, you will know that you have to act when there is a consensus of criticism.

Critical readers

This raises a difficult and troublesome problem. When do you show your work to other people, and which people should they be?

Writing a full-length book can be a lonely business, and it is understandable that one should seek some response in the process, but this should be carefully thought through. You should also ask yourself this question: why are you showing your work to the other person? Do you really want genuine criticism or judgment, or simply affirmation? There is nothing wrong with wanting affirmation, but the problem is this: what happens if you don't get it? Will that sap your energy and damage your morale? If so, it might be better to press on to the end before showing anything to anyone.

The process of writing can be easily swerved off-course by lukewarm or negative remarks when you are mid-way. Sometimes the writer needs to cross a patch of indifferent writing to arrive at the part that will stay in, but that does not mean that the indifferent writing did not have to be done. Someone else saying at this point, 'I didn't find this very gripping, to be honest,' is the last thing you want.

must know

Work in progress

Think carefully about the timing of showing work in progress to anyone. Much fiction writing is bungled, to one degree or another, until it finds its overall form right at the end. Much writing en route is exploratory; it should not be treated as though it were finalized.

As to reading your own work out loud, this can only help. Inadequate punctuation, unimaginative vocabulary or slack syntax – all these should shout out to you if you read from the page. (This form of correction is unfortunately impossible in public libraries.)

Researching fiction

There are no rules here, except one. The research must improve the writing that finally ends up on the page. If it doesn't, it should be dispensed with ruthlessly. This might seem obvious, but it often isn't. The word 'Cut' is frequently used during the editorial process to hack away research the writer himself couldn't bear to part with, because too much time went into making all those notes.

Research has two main functions: to give the writing its necessary credibility, and to provide the writer with a necessary stimulus. Graham Greene would set off to another country in pursuit of stimulation; some writers go to the library. A good writer should be able to use almost anything as an object of research: old coins, postcards, books (obviously), maps, photographs, letters, recordings, conversations. The more material the objects are, the better.

When Flaubert wrote his *Three Tales*, he borrowed the stuffed parrot from the local museum in Rouen so that he could look at it constantly while describing Félicité's growing adoration of the bird. He claimed that virtually the whole of the inspiration for another of the stories, 'Saint Julien the Hospitalier', was provided by a single plate-glass window in Rouen Cathedral. It is often a question of the intense use to which a resource is put, rather than the actual extent of the resources. Fiction is, after all, imaginative writing. Everything must finally work on the page.

On the other hand, the fiction writer must try to get it right as much as possible. Frank Kermode has spoken of 'the necessary omniscience of the novelist'. He was writing of John Updike at the time, but what he was indicating was the duty of the fiction writer to acquire all the available facts that might help in the evocation of reality. This could require a lot of legwork. If you are going to write a fictionalized account of Darwin aboard the *Beagle*, then you might need to consider travelling to the Galapagos Islands. If you are Iain Sinclair, you might walk for 20 miles around London.

Thomas Mann wrote a book called *Genesis of A Novel*, which was his account of how he had worked on *Doctor Faustus*. It is a fascinating account of how a writer uses everything to hand. Mann had created a modern composer in his novel, but he still didn't know how to make him entirely credible. His required research here consisted of a relationship with the theorist and music critic, Theodor Adorno. It turned out that all the crucial questions he needed to ask could be answered by this man. So Mann asked them, at every available opportunity. Research for fiction is often a form of opportunism. Take what is offered, and make use of it.

This whole subject perhaps raises another question about fiction: to what extent does it look discredited if it is shown to be based on faulty historical information? There might be no straightforward answer to that question. When

must know

Howlers

Whatever you write about you have a responsibility to observe accurately. If you cannot do this at first-hand, then you must do it by research. Howlers in fiction erode the reader's confidence in everything else.

must know

Balancing research

Research is that which is necessary to achieve the type of fiction being written. Less than that will make the text inadequate; more will overburden it. James Joyce plagued his friends and relatives for more and more details about the topography and street-life of Dublin. Why? Because obsessing over the topography of the loved and hated city permitted the working of his imagination. The extent of the research is always what is specifically needed for this particular piece of fiction, neither more nor less.

Kurt Vonnegut wrote *Slaughterhouse 5*, he used for historical evidence a book by David Irving on the bombing of Dresden, a book which has since been proved to be an unreliable source. This means that Vonnegut's statistics for the casualties after the fire-bombing of Dresden are seriously exaggerated. All this is made even more bizarre because Vonnegut was actually a prisoner in Dresden at the time of the fire-bombing, but then he could hardly have been expected to have counted up all the bodies himself. Does this discredit the book as fiction? No, but if someone had used tainted historical evidence to write fiction claiming that the Holocaust never happened, that would surely draw the fiction itself into question.

There is a coda to all this, which might be as curious as anything in Vonnegut's own fiction. In *Mother Night* he portrayed a man in an Israeli prison cell, a man accused of broadcasting Nazi propaganda during the war: Howard W. Campbell, Jr. David Irving was until recently in a prison cell outside Vienna, having been tried and convicted for Holocaust denial, which is to say, issuing Nazi propaganda. The text we read when we read *Mother Night* is the accused man's *Memoirs*. David Irving apparently spent his time in jail writing his memoirs. Sometimes it seems that Oscar Wilde was right: life does imitate art.

We should always remember that the function of research in fiction might not be to provide plot or character, but to make invented plot and character credible. Let us look again at the story by Borges entitled 'Deutsches Requiem'. In that story we are told that Linde receives his ultimate challenge after he has been appointed subdirector of the concentration camp at Tarnowitz in 1941. There is actually a place called Tarnowitz in Silesia, but there was never a Nazi concentration camp there. It is plausible, though, that there might have been. It is situated in a credible region at a credible time. This is the function of research. Had the camp been placed in, say, Spain, then it would not have been credible.

Linde receives into his lethal care David Jerusalem, a poor but eminent Jewish poet. So great is Linde's admiration for this man's work that he has learnt by heart a substantial part of his poem *Tse Yang, Painter of Tigers*. Linde, to expunge the last traces of unworthy compassion he finds within himself, tortures the poet until he goes mad and subsequently kills himself. He says how in his eyes Jerusalem was no longer a man, not even a Jew; he'd transmuted somehow into what Linde calls 'a detested zone of my soul.' In ensuring his death, Linde is killing something in himself. Jerusalem's extinction has rid Linde of all that he finds detestable in his own humanity: compassion, mercy, pity, identification with the other's suffering. In one sense, a Nietzschean sense in fact, he has ceased to be human. And this was his aim.

He would claim that he has risen above humanity. The prosecutors at the Nuremburg Trials would have insisted that he had sunk beneath it, but Linde, as he makes plain at the beginning, refused to testify on his own behalf. He will not deign to defend himself. He permits the charges to be laid in silence. What will be, will be. He even accepts the defeat of Germany in a fatalistic hymn to necessity. There is a last irony fashioned into the story: it is possible,

now you do it

Write a summary

It is often necessary to write a brief summary or synopsis of your book. This 'author's summary' is often used on the cover. It should discard all inessentials and emphasize what might be of significance to any potential publisher or reader. Try writing 200 words. Make sure every sentence increases interest, rather than decreasing it.

must know

Keeping a notebook

There should always be a large file into which you put whatever might seem relevant for the writing of the book you are working on: newspaper cuttings, photographs, references to other books. You should always have a notebook in your pocket or your bag, in which you can write down thoughts and observations as they occur. As the work intensifies, this notebook will probably need to lie beside your bed all night.

so a (fictional) editor's note informs us, that David Jerusalem never existed. There is no record of him elsewhere. As he explains laconically, it is conceivable that 'David Jerusalem' is perhaps a combined symbol, which has brought several individuals together. And then we recall that there was no such concentration camp as Tarnowitz. There never was any such person as David Jerusalem. But a great deal else in the story is real, which is to say historical, and the mind of Linde becomes all too real to us in that hybridized reality we call fiction. No rules ever dictate what is the necessary research, but carelessness is not permissible.

If, for example, someone were to write a novel which put the philosopher Ludwig Wittgenstein in a Cambridge debating society at a time when he was actually fighting for his native Austria on the Eastern Front, this does not constitute fictional liberty – unless the writer makes it plain to us that the displacement is a knowing one – but rather intellectual slovenliness, of a sort that should make us dubious about the trustworthiness of any such author.

Submitting fiction for publication

The first rule here is: don't – not as long as a single word can be improved. Long before sending anything off, the writer must draft, re-draft and re-draft again; seek the opinion of people you trust. Tell them to be ruthlessly honest.

Any place that receives work for publication will be staffed by busy people, who are seldom sentimental about their work. A misplaced adjective in the first paragraph might be enough to send the typescript back in its stamped addressed envelope there and then. If this should happen, you have already deleted one possible destination for your work, and there is no one but yourself to blame.

You should make the writing as close to perfect as possible before it lands on any editor's desk. People in publishing do not regard themselves as unpaid educationalists, and they tend not to provide their proofreading services free.

Think carefully about where you are sending your work and why. Find out as much information as possible about the agency or publisher you are approaching. Look carefully at the last section in the *Writers' and Artists' Yearbook*, to learn as much as you can. What sort of work is accepted? On what terms? Are unsolicited typescripts welcome, or not? If not, then there is not much point sending one. Is work only accepted through literary agents? If so, and you don't have one, then you had better look elsewhere.

How to send your work for consideration

If there is a specified protocol for the submission of work, then follow it to the letter. If not, follow these rules.

- Work should only be sent electronically by prior arrangement.
- Any typescript should be double-spaced in a legible typeface, and with a font size no smaller than twelve. Never use fancy Gothic typefaces. Even using one in the privacy of your own home should make you re-consider your seriousness as a writer.
- Always include a stamped addressed envelope for the return of the typescript.

now you do it

Researching trends

Don't think that following trends is a route to publication. It might be. On the other hand, it might not. Is that really what you want, in any case? Look at what is in bookshops, obviously; read the review pages of serious newspapers and periodicals. Then, when you have done all that, remind yourself that you have to do something no one else has quite done. Combine your experience, your passion, your unique research and turn them into an original book. Why bother writing a second-hand version of Margaret Atwood or Martin Amis? For the same money, we can buy the original books they wrote. So why fuss about with clones? Fiction isn't fashion. It's far more important than that, which is why it lasts so much longer.

must know

Rejection

Rejection is part of a writer's life. If you cannot cope with it, then you are not going to survive. Remember that rejection, not once but many times, was the fate of most writers at the beginning of their careers.

• It might be better to get used to the idea of the return of such typescripts, because it happens to most fiction writers, particularly at the beginning of their careers.

• The typescript or electronic attachment should always be accompanied by a synopsis, no more than a page long. This should give a lucid, and dispassionate, account of the book in question. Avoid all self-praising adjectives. Do not tell the recipient that this is a 'passionate and harrowing' account of whatever; they'll make up their own minds about that soon enough. The synopsis should

Advertising yourself

The covering letter you write to an agent or publisher might be all they read. If your first paragraph is dull or ungrammatical, your manuscript might be tossed straight on to the reject pile. Make your letter an interesting read in itself. Explain what it is about the book that might make anyone want to read it. If there are any factors about your life or career that are relevant, mention them. Do not, however, sound cocky or self-important. Agents and publishers spend a lot of their lives dealing with people who are 'absolutely convinced' of the importance of their work. Such absolute conviction, sadly, often remains unreciprocated. Let writing be convincing enough in its own right. That is the real battle. That is what this book is all about.

be shown to a number of trusted readers before you finally send it off. It should be brisk, highly readable, and free from self-importance.

• Always be courteous and polite in your dealings with agents and publishers, even if your courtesy is not always reciprocated. It's no good ranting that no one's paying any attention to you. You are pursuing them, not the other way around.

Remember, finally, no one asked you to do it. It's often a long haul. It also happens to be one of the most rewarding activities known to humanity, when real achievements finally emerge. Read the letters of Gustave Flaubert in the Penguin edition, or an autobiographical account of the writer's life such as Paul Auster's *Hand to Mouth*. What they both display is the sheer graft and grind of writing serious fiction. There is much pain involved for those who are serious. There are no short-cuts.

We do it because we need to, and want to, not for any immediate reward. On the other hand, if immediate rewards arrive, don't refuse them.

The ultimate reward for this painstaking, laborious, quirky business is the knowledge that you have managed to create a genuine reality through your writing. Words on the page can make a person live, bring a voice alive, resurrect a destroyed location, re-activate history.

It is not easy, but if you can create a piece of writing that you know has done any of these things, then it is a remarkable achievement.

want to know more?

• ***The Writers' and Artists' Yearbook*, published by A & C Black, and *The Writers' Handbook*, published by Macmillan, are both revised annually. They list the main UK publishers and agents, with a note about the areas they specialize in and the way they want submissions to be presented.**

• **You'll find listings of university creative writing courses in the pages of both the *Yearbook* and the *Handbook*.**

• **If you don't want to commit to a full year's course, consider doing a shorter course with the Arvon Foundation www.arvonfoundation.org.**

• **You'll find a list of useful websites for writers on page 181.**

Further information

Select bibliography

Atwood, Margaret, *The Penelopiad* (Edinburgh: Canongate, 2006)

Auster, Paul, *Hand to Mouth* (London: Faber, 1998)

Banville, John, *Doctor Copernicus* (London: Picador, 1998)

Barker, Pat, *Regeneration* (London: Penguin, 1992)

Beckett, Samuel, *The Trilogy* (London: John Calder, 1994)

Borges, Jorge Luis, *Collection Fictions* (London: Allen Lane, 2000)

Carroll, Lewis, *The Annotated Alice* (ed. Martin Gardner) (London: Penguin, 1977)

Cook, Elizabeth, *Achilles* (London: Methuen, 2001)

Coupe, Laurence, *Myth* (London and New York: Routledge, 1997)

Crumey, Andrew, *Mobius Dick* (London: Picador, 2004)

Dawson, Jill, *Wild Boy* (London: Hodder, 2003)

De Lillo, Don, *Libra* (London: Penguin, 1989)

Dudman, Clare, *Wegener's Jigsaw* (London: Sceptre, 2003)

Flaubert, Gustave, *Selected Letters*, ed. Geoffrey Wall (London: Penguin, 1997)

Gardner, John, *Grendel* (London: Gollancz, 2004)

Gibson, William, *Neuromancer* (London: HarperCollins, 1995)

Josipovici, Gabriel, *The Singer on the Shore* (Manchester: Carcanet, 2006)

Joyce, James, *Ulysses* (London: Penguin, 2000)

Lodge, David, *The Art of Fiction* (London: Penguin, 1992)

Mann, Thomas, *Doctor Faustus* (London: Vintage, 1996)

Melville, Herman, *Moby Dick* (Oxford: OUP, 1999)

Mitchell, David, *Ghostwritten* (London: Hodder, 1999)

Moorcock, Michael, *The Vengeance of Rome* (London: Cape, 2006). (See also the other three titles in this trilogy: *Byzantium Endures*, *The Laughter of Carthage* and *Jerusalem Commands*)

Nabokov, Vladimir, *Pale Fire* (London: Penguin, 2000)

Newman, Jenny, *Going In* (London: Hamish Hamilton, 1994)

Newman, Jenny, Edmund Cusick and Aileen La Tourette (eds), *The Writer's Workbook* (London: Hodder, 2004)

Proulx, Annie, *The Shipping News* (London: Fourth Estate, 1994)

Sinclair, Iain (ed.), *London: City of Disappearances* (London: Hamish Hamilton, 2006)

Swift, Jonathan, *Gulliver's Travels* (Oxford: OUP, 2005)

Vonnegut, Kurt, *Mother Night* (London: Vintage, 2000)
Wallace, David Foster, *Brief Interviews with Hideous Men* (London: Abacus, 2000)
White, Tony, *Foxy-T* (London: Faber, 2004)
Zivkovic, Zoran, *Hidden Camera* (Dalkey Archive Press, 2005)

Dictionaries

The Oxford English Dictionary is an invaluable resource for any writer. It comes in many shapes and sizes. No version shorter than the *Concise Oxford Dictionary* should be used. Etymological dictionaries are also very useful. The Chambers volume is invaluable. *The Cassell Dictionary of Slang* is useful for demotic phrases and intonations. There are now a multitude of thesauruses apart from Roget, but the original has managed to retain its charm.

Directories

An extensive listing of societies, organizations, prizes, publishers and agents can be found in *Writers' and Artists' Yearbook* (published by A & C Black) and *The Writers' Handbook* (published by Macmillan), which are updated each year.

Useful websites

- www.writersservices.com
  The Writers' and Artists' Yearbook online
- www.writersresources.co.uk
  Advice and information for aspiring and professional writers
- www.thebookseller.com
  Find out what publishers are thinking about
- http://books.guardian.co.uk/originalfiction
  Original fiction published online
- www.booksurgepublishing.com
  Self-publishing and print-on-demand services
- www.lulu.com/uk
  Publish and sell your own book at this site
- www.complete-review.com/saloon
  Opinions and commentary on literary matters
- www.readysteadybook.com
  Articles, book reviews and interviews
- www.lrb.co.uk
  The online version of the *London Review of Books*, for subscribers
- www.spikemagazine.com
  Interviews and book reviews with writers, musicians, artists and publishers

Useful addresses

Society of Authors
84 Drayton Gardens, London SW10 9SB
Tel: 020-7373 6642
email: info@societyofauthors.org
website: www.societyofauthors.org
General Secretary: Mark Le Fanu

The Society of Authors is an independent trade union, representing writers' interests in all aspects of the writing profession, particularly publishing.

Membership is open to writers with a full-length work published or accepted for publication in the UK; also for those who have had stories published. Associate membership is available for a year for those who have been offered a contract which requires them to contribute financially to publication; a relevant vetting service is offered.

The Arvon Foundation
2nd floor
42A Buckingham Palace Road
London SW1W 0RE
Tel: 020 7931 7611
website: www.arvonfoundation.org

Offers the chance to attend week-long courses and work with well-known authors. For beginners through to experienced writers, covering novels, poetry, drama, writing for children, even songwriting.

Acknowledgements

The author is grateful to the following for their help: Brian Baker, Andrew Hedgecock, Stephen Lloyd, Anthony Rudolf, Bernard Sharratt. Many of the ideas here were first formulated when the author was part of the Royal Literary Fund's innovative Fellowship Scheme.

Glossary of fictional terms

Beginning
The beginning of the writing is not the same as the beginning of the book. The beginning of the writing is whatever provides the prompt a writer needs to set out on the journey which ends in the construction of a completed narrative. The beginning of the finished work of fiction is often not settled until the end of the writing process. Sometimes it is only when the theme has been explored fully that the writer can see exactly which words need to be employed to state the given theme to its greatest effect on the first page.

Causality
This is the realm of order; the kingdom of rules. Here what can happen must happen, and everything that happens can be explained. It is the principle of causality which ultimately makes all plots explicable; an excess of it makes the writing mechanical. *See* Contingency.

Characterization
Everything we read about a character adds to that composite of description and report which we call characterization. The clothes someone wears; their normal facial expression; the way they speak; what others say of them: all of this ultimately adds up to characterization. The character the writer presents is therefore a matter of selection. For this reason, the initial descriptive details need to be chosen with great care. Fiction frequently achieves its characterizations through metonymy.

Coincidence
Two or more things happening in relation to each other are described as coincidental. In one sense all plotting is based on

coincidence. Why does this person meet that one, leading to the relationship which forms the basis of the plot? The whole of the plot of Evelyn Waugh's *Scoop* is based on the coincidence of two people named Boot; this coincidence is then exploited for its comic potential. David Mitchell uses an extraordinary series of coincidences to link the various internal plots of his novel *Ghostwritten*. Such a profusion of coincidence, particularly if the coincidences are happy, is known as serendipity. It needs to be employed with great caution in fiction, or it can lead to sentimentality.

Contingency

This is the relentless force that challenges causality. Contingency describes everything which might happen but doesn't have to; it might not happen, but it could. Contingency announces the arrival of the unexpected. It introduces happenstance and serendipity. It is what brings plots to life, though an excess of it brings inchoherence.

Defamiliarization

This is a technique whereby the writer sees reality through a slightly adjusted optic, and thereby renders the familiar strange. Normally the process of our perceptions operates the other way around: we encounter the exotic and make it familiar. We give human names to inhuman things. We call the devastating hurricane that struck New Orleans 'Katrina'. In this manner we 'familiarize' a destructive force of nature. When a writer describes something so that we see it afresh, as though we had never seen it before, that is defamiliarization.

Ending

The modern writer needs to bear in mind that everything does not have to be settled, completed, scored, rounded-off. The excessive completion of the endings of Dickens now strikes us as artificial. All endings are cuts as much as resolutions. Don't try to convert all contingency into causality – that leads to sentimentality and excessive symmetry.

Figures of speech

We all use figures of speech all the time, without really thinking about it. Metaphors, similes, personification, under-statement, hyperbole, metonymy – these are a part of the richness which the language affords. They permit the contraction of a variety of information and perception into individual images. They are potent because of the economy of expression they afford. So on the first page of *Moby Dick* Ishmael informs us that he goes to sea 'whenever it is a damp drizzly November in my soul'. This is a metaphor, taking its colour from meteorology. It conveys a lot of information briefly and succinctly. It achieves its power, as metaphors usually do, from a process of defamiliarization. No careful writer can afford to employ figures of speech carelessly; if such figures arrive second-hand and well-used, then they are already clichés.

Irony

Irony exploits a fracture between surface meaning and the intimations of a different meaning lying behind or beneath the surface of a text. At its most rudimentary we have verbal irony. 'You're a genius aren't you?' I say to a friend who has recently perpetrated a particular idiocy. A more sophisticated form of irony in fiction is structural irony; here the work is constructed in such a manner that we gradually begin to understand we are observing a distancing principle which effectively highlights or italicizes the text before us; it makes us question the validity of the words. A classic instance is Swift's 'Modest Proposal', whose measured language soon reveals itself to be in fact recommending infanticide in Ireland. Nabokov's *Pale Fire* is another instance of structural irony. We are presented with a poem by the dead American poet John Shade; then we are given a commentary on this poem by the editor Charles Kinbote, whose radically deformed reading of the original text alerts us, page by page, to Kinbote's insanity.

In irony the whole text refuses to endorse the stated import of local parts of itself. In certain 'postmodern' writers the whole text puts itself into question, and we enter that sphere which philosophers refer to as 'infinitized irony', where no corrective is strong enough to remedy the dissonance out of which the original irony arose.

Magic Realism

This is a contemporary fictional mode which allows the fabulous to re-enter the adult world of fiction. The ancient grammarians had said that fiction stood midway between fable and history; it had some of the freedom of the one, but required the evidential credibility of the other. The magic realists have re-claimed for themselves much more of the freedom of the original fabulists and legend-makers. They want the fantastic and the surreal as a part of their text. Major practitioners in this mode include Gabriel García Márquez, Salman Rushdie, Günter Grass and Italo Calvino.

Metonymy

(Note that metonymy is here used to include synechedoche, a usage that has become increasingly common.)

Fiction is as dependent on metonymy as poetry is on metaphor. So what is it? In its most basic form it is used to mean employing a part, or an attribute, for the whole of the thing referred to. If I say the prows come over the waves (meaning the boats approach), or the factory hands are massing (meaning the workers are on strike), then I am using metonymy. But the meaning of the term goes farther than this. Metaphor makes connections between different realms; it holds together aspects of different spheres by combining parallel characteristics in a single image. Marianne Moore says of a swan that it turns and reconnoitres like a battleship. Here she has brought together two different realms of perception in a simile (which is a loosely bound metaphor). Metonymy makes its connections not in this vertical, inter-category manner, but horizontally, by describing the surrounding events and objects of the person being described. If I give a description of the way someone always punches his hat with great vigour before putting it on his head, or how another person arranges papers, pens, erasers, pencils, on a desk before writing a letter, then I am using metonymy as a form of description. It is a characteristic fictional device. I do not have to describe someone's impatience: I simply describe the incessant drumming of their fingers on a table. By this means I describe a state of mind without having to state it. Metonymy permits the vivid conveyance of character and mood by obliquity. At the beginning of Saul Bellow's novel *Herzog*, a loaf of bread is described. A rat has left the shape of its body inside it; Herzog then eats what is left. This metonymic device conveys to us the disregard for the normal conventions of life and hygiene which now characterize the distant spiritual and psychological state of the protagonist.

Narrative voice

The voice with which fiction speaks to us establishes its authority, its intimacy, its nearness or distance, its credentials for being believed. The ironically detached voice of Jane Austen allows for a distancing manoeuvre whereby we see all the characters with a certain dispassionate, even forensic, objectivity. The normal voicings are: first-person, third-person, and the free indirect style, which allows for an alteration between the two. Occasionally a writer will use the second person – 'You do this, you do that' – as Lorrie Moore does in one of the stories in *Self-Help*, but it is a difficult voicing to sustain for any length of time, and it is rare.

Plot

Plot is the sequencing of history through narrative. It is not the order in which things actually happened, but the sequence of revelations about those happenings in a piece of writing. First we see the corpse, then we move backwards through history and motivations, partial evidence and biased testimony, until we come to understand how the corpse came to be lying there on the carpet, covered in blood. If plot were synonymous with history - Reginald shot Charles out of jealousy and that's why his corpse is lying on the carpet - then 'plotting' effectively disappears, and we are left instead with a chronicle, and chronicles are famously free from suspense and tension. All fictional writing is a form of revelation, which uncovers its interior truth gradually. We only want to read on because we don't know everything immediately. Fiction often follows the advice of Polonius in *Hamlet*: 'by indirections' it 'finds directions out'.

Serendipity

There is an old Persian fairy-tale called 'The Three Princes of Serendip'. These fellows were constantly sallying forth to discover unexpected blessings and unanticipated delights. The word Serendip was derived from the Arabic word for present day Sri Lanka, and it was borrowed by Horace Walpole in a letter of 1754 and turned into our present word. So serendipity is that condition, by extension, of happy coincidences, unexpected turns of good fortune. It should be used consciously, even self-consciously, by the modern writer of fiction. It should never be employed, as it frequently was by Dickens, to resolve magically an otherwise intractable plot.

Unreliable narrator

A voice within a text (which may also be the entire voice of the text) which we begin to distrust because of a growing sense of dissonance between what this voice is telling us and our own expectations in regard to, or knowledge of, reality. We conclude that the narrative voice of Edgar Allan Poe's 'The Tell-Tale Heart' belongs to a madman because he insists that a murdered man's heart carries on a life of its own. We conclude that Charles Kinbote, the editor in Nabokov's *Pale Fire* is an unreliable narrator because of his patently demented and self-regarding reading of John Shade's poem.

Things are more complex in Henry James's *The Turn of the Screw*, where the governess sees things, and sees children seeing things, which we as readers begin to doubt. Have the children in fact been corrupted by malign forces, or is her hysterical mind engaged in a process of twisted imaginings? Henry James does not provide any 'authorial direction': instead he leaves the reader to judge.

Verisimilitude

This is the truthfulness of writing within its given form. Forms of writing dictate different types of possibility. If I speak in the first-person in a story and I start to tell you with great certitude what other people are thinking, then I must either explain how I know, or leave you to assume that I am possibly insane – which is to say an unreliable narrator. The word means 'an appearance of truth'; in fiction an appearance of truth is truth, unless it is being subverted by verbal or structural irony.

Index

A
anamorphic projection 103, 154, 155
Arvon Foundation 177, 182
Atwood, Margaret
The Penelopiad 30
Auden, W.H. 77
Austen, Jane 84, 187
Pride and Prejudice 11-12, 20, 99
Auster, Paul *Hand to Mouth* 177
B
Bakhtin 84, 85, 86, 90, 95, 130, 145, 150
Baldwin, James 87
Banville, John 144, 146
Barker, Pat *Regeneration* 15-16, 30, 32, 42, 67
Baudelaire, Charles 147
Beckett, Samuel 36, 43-4, 58, 115
Malone Dies 112
The Unnameable 93
Waiting for Godot 33
Beerbohm, Max 108
Behan, Brendan *Borstal Boy* 44
Belloc, Hilaire 108
Bellow, Saul
Adventures of Augie March 90
Herzog 19, 102, 187
Benjamin, Walter 66, 67
Bennett, Alan *Talking Heads* 69
Beowulf 50, 138
bestseller lists 95
Bible 71-2, 122
biography, miniaturized 73-5
Blake, William 48, 147
Bloom, Harold 118
Borges, Jorge Luis 137
'Death and the Compass' 75
'Deutsches Requiem' 68-70, 172-3
'Funes, His Memory' 160
'On Exactitude in Science' 159-60
'The Memory of Shakespeare' 80
Brontë, Charlotte *Jane Eyre* 90
Brontë, Emily *Wuthering Heights* 40, 42
Brown, George Mackay 129
Browning, Robert 68
Bulgakov, Mikhail *The Master and Margarita* 147
Burns, Robert 51
Burroughs, William 93-4
C
Calvino, Italo 186
Camus, Albert *The Outsider* 19
Capote, Truman *In Cold Blood* 90
Carroll, Lewis *Alice in Wonderland* 17-18
Carter, Angela 36
'Overture and Incidental Music for *A Midsummer Night's Dream*' 81, 123
causality 31, 85, 156, 183
character 15-25
archetypes 161
character study exercise 149
development 76, 79
in setting 41
Chekhov 81
Chesterton, G.K. *Father Brown Stories* 77
chronology 30
classic realist fiction 12, 34
classification of novels 87-8, 129-30
cliché 48, 50, 162, 186
coincidence 132-7, 183-4
Coleridge 14
composition 24-5, 61
contingency 84-5, 93-4, 156, 184
Cook, Elizabeth *Achilles* 121-2
Coppola, Francis Ford
The Conversation 157
Crumey, Andrew *Möbius Dick* 134, 144
cynicism 104
D
Dante 121
The Divine Comedy 33
Dawson, *Jill Wild Boy* 40, 41, 42, 125-6
defamiliarization 48-51, 133, 184
DeLillo, Don 157, 167
Libra 91, 154
Mao II 157
Running Dog 156
dénouement 36
detective plot exercise 29
detective story 75
dialectics 71
dialogic 89
dictionaries 48, 51, 55, 181
displacement 139-143
Doctorow, E.L. 124
Billy Bathgate 125
Book of Daniel 124
Ragtime 91, 124
Welcome to Hard Times 124
documentary fiction 91
Dos Passos, John *USA* 91
Dostoyevsky
Notes from Underground 19
The Devils 146
Doyle, Arthur Conan 71
drama of confinement 44, 137-9
Dudman, Clare
Wegener's Jigsaw 146
Duggan, Alfred 127
Duncan, Glen *I, Lucifer* 147
duologue 70-72, 81
Durrell, Lawrence
Alexandria Quartet 144
E
Einstein 40, 128, 144
Eliot, George
Middlemarch 44, 125
Eliot, T.S. 93
endings 34-5, 135, 153, 184-5
epic 84, 86, 138
epiphany 72-3, 75
episodic novel 90
experiential writing 147-9
F
Faulkner, William 45
As I Lay Dying 88
Fielding, Henry *Shamela* 88
Fields, W.C., comedy films 115
figures of speech 49-50, 61, 62, 185

Finch, Peter 105
Fitzgerald, Scott 'Basil: The Freshest Boy' 79
Flaubert, Gustave
letters 177
Madame Bovary 74
Three Tales 74-5, 170
Ford, Ford Madox 51
Forster, E.M. 75
Forsyth, Frederick *Day of the Jackal* 32
fragmentation 34
free indirect style 20, 22, 23-4, 94, 102
Freud, Sigmund 18, 78, 114, 115
Civilisation and its Discontents 92
Jokes and Their Relation to the Unconscious 108
G
García Márquez, Gabriel 186
Gardner, John *Grendel* 50, 68, 138, 154-5
Genesis, Book of 148
genre
boundaries 87
novel's cannibalization of 86
categorization 95
requirement 35
subversion 33
gesture 152
ghost stories 78, 80
Gibson, William *Neuromancer* 142
Grass, Günter 186
Greene, Graham 44, 128, 170
Gulliver's Travels 140-41, 155
H
Hardy, Thomas 45, 51
Heller, Joseph *Catch 22* 17
Hemingway 58, 63
In Our Time; Men Without Women 34
'The Short Happy Life of Francis Macomber' 79
'Soldier's Home' 67
historical novel 15
history 124-8
Homer 67
Odyssey 120
Iliad 84, 121
Hooke, Robert *Micrographia* 140
humour 85, 108-15
concealing vulnerability 115
dissonance 108, 109-10, 112
hierarchy of significance 112-13
inevitability 109
insults 112
juxtaposition 110
linguistic precision 111-12
I
imagery in language 50, 51
interviewing characters exercise 23
intolerable gift 162
ironic perception exercise 102
irony 94, 98-105, 156, 185
and sincerity 99
between characters 104-5
escaping 99, 100
generating suspicion 103
in poems 105
modern dilemma 100-102
off-setting 104
subtle 105
verbal and structural 102-3
Irwin, Robert *Satan Wants Me* 147
J
James, Henry 30, 34-5, 63
The Turn of the Screw 80, 189
James, M.R. 78
Johnson, B.S. 94
Jonson, Ben 71-2
Joyce, James 72-3, 115, 172
Dubliners 73
Finnegans Wake 36, 93
Portrait of the Artist as a Young Man 13-14, 73, 90, 148
Ulysses 33, 58, 93, 119, 122, 148-9
Jung, Carl 80
K
Kafka *Metamorphosis* 33, 70
Kermode, Frank 171
Kertesz, André *On Reading* 87
Kierkegaard 35
Kipling, Rudyard
'Proofs of Holy Writ' 71, 80-81
Koch, Kenneth 105
Kraus, Karl 150
L
language
as fabric of writing 51
balance of Anglo-Saxon and Romance words 54
etymology, fossil poetry 55
Lawrence, D.H. *Lady Chatterley's Lover* 152
Leven, Jeremy *Satan: A Case Study* 147
Levi, Primo *The Periodic Table* 145
location in time and place 43-5
M
Magic Realism 49, 90, 136, 162, 163, 186
Mann, Thomas
Doctor Faustus 146
Genesis of A Novel 171
Magic Mountain 138
McEwan, Ian 144
McKee, Robert *Story* 37
Melville, Herman 150, 151
Billy Budd, Foretopman 89, 101
Moby Dick 10-11, 12, 19, 122, 123, 158, 185
metaphor and simile 49-50
metonymy 186-7
Milton 123
Paradise Lost 147
miserabilism 112
Mitchell, David
Ghostwritten 31, 136, 185
modern experience 66-8
difficulty in communicating 66-7
fragmentation 67
Modern Movement 14
monologue 68-70
montage 34, 66, 67
Moorcock, Michael *Pyat Quartet* 127-8
Moore, Lorrie *Self-Help* 187
Moore, Marianne 187
More, Thomas *Utopia* 139
myth 33, 118-23
N
Nabokov *Pale Fire* 86, 89, 102, 185
Naipaul, V.S. 128
narrative bias 22
narrative dynamism 62
narrative impulse 89

narrative voice 12, 13, 20-24, 25, 187-8
Newman, Jenny *Going In* 149
Nietzsche 105
'The Use and Abuse of History' 160
novel
as an omnivorous form 86
characteristics of 84-7
defying definition 93, 94
illimitability 87-9
types of 90-91
novella form 79, 91-2
nonfiction novel 91
O
obscenity 92
omniscient narrator 12, 21
opening 10-14, 161-2
Orwell, George
essays 63
Nineteen Eighty-four 142
Owen, Wilfred 15
P
pace 28
paranoid fiction 91, 103, 153-9
pastiche 127
pattern-recognition 50
place 128-31
planning 166
plot 188
action 28-9
alienation 34
archetypal 32, 121
coincidence 31
fragmentation 34
modern 33
moving towards resolution 35-7
psychology 31
selective revelation 29
Poe, Edgar Allan
'The Murders in the Rue Morgue' 75
'The Tell-Tale Heart' 68, 69, 70, 189
poets 62
Pound, Ezra 48, 51
Powell, Anthony *O How the Wheel Becomes It* 133
precision of language 111
Pritchett, V.S. 63
Proulx, Annie *The Shipping News* 22
Proust, Marcel
Remembrance of Things Past 90
psychological novel 90
psychology 30, 149-53
punctuation 56-8
Pynchon, Thomas 91
The Crying of Lot 49 36, 144, 154, 155-6, 159
R
Rankin, Ian 35
reality, unexpectedness of 85
redrafting 167
regional novels 131
rejection 176
religion 147-9
research 45, 94, 170-74
resources 95
revelation 73
revising 168-9
Rhys, Jean *Wide Sargasso Sea* 88
Richardson, Samuel
Pamela 88
Robinson Crusoe 138, 140
Rolfe, Frederick *Hadrian VII* 158
Roth, Philip 93, 94
American Pastoral 92
Sabbath's Theatre 92, 93
The Human Stain 86, 92
Rushdie, Salman 186
'The Prophet's Hair' 49, 162
S
Sassoon, Siegfried 15
selection 158, 159-63
selective revelation 29
sentences 58-63
serendipity 135-6, 188
sex 92
science fiction 140-43
Shakespeare, William 71-2, 80-81, 122
Macbeth 152
Othello 67
The Tempest 49, 51
short story as puzzle 75-8
Sinclair, Iain 171
Downriver 129-30
Smith, Adam 13
social novel 90
Society of Authors 182
Solzhenitsyn *Cancer Ward; One Day in the Life of Ivan Denisovich* 138
Sophocles *Oedipus Rex* 29, 133
Stone, Oliver JFK 157
stream-of-consciousness 103
storytelling 89
Strachey, Lytton *Eminent Victorians* 127
submitting for publication 174-7
suspense 28
Swanson, David *The Paranoid* 154
Swift, Graham
Last Orders 88
Gulliver's Travels 89
Swift, Jonathan 'A Modest Proposal' 98, 100, 185
synopsis 176
syntax 55-6
T
Thackeray, William Makepeace *Vanity Fair* 85
Theroux, Paul 128
Thurber, James 118
Tolstoy *Anna Karenina* 162
Tournier, Michel *Friday* 88
trends 175
Truffaut, François 41
Twain, Mark *Tom Sawyer; Huckleberry Finn* 19
U
Updike, John 171
universal struggle 13
unreliable narrator 68-9, 70, 80, 150, 188-9
V
verisimilitude 35, 137, 189
Virgil 121
The Aeneid 33
vivid settings 44
voice and character 24
Vonnegut, Kurt 37, 87-8, 143
Mother Night 135, 172
Slaughterhouse 5 172
W
Wallace, David Foster 81
Brief Interviews with Hideous Men 24, 66, 150
Walpole, Horace 135, 188
Waugh, Evelyn 44, 113, 128
The Ordeal of Gilbert Pinfold 158
Scoop 132, 133, 185
Welsh, Irvine
Trainspotting 33
word awareness 51-3
word processing 167-8
Writers' and Artists' Yearbook, The 175, 177
Writers' Handbook, The 177